THE MODERN HISTORIAN

THE
MODERN HISTORIAN

by

C. H. Williams

Professor of History in the
University of London

THOMAS NELSON AND SONS, Ltd.
LONDON, EDINBURGH, PARIS, MELBOURNE
TORONTO, AND NEW YORK

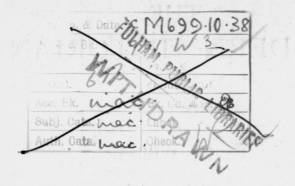
First published, July 1938

ACKNOWLEDGMENTS

I wish to make grateful acknowledgment to the following authors for the ready permission they granted me to make quotations from their works: Professor G. N. Clark, Dr. G. P. Gooch, Dr. A. F. Pollard, Professor F. M. Powicke, Professor R. H. Tawney, Professor A. Hamilton Thompson, Professor A. J. Toynbee, Professor G. M. Trevelyan, and to the publishers—Messrs. Bell, Messrs. Constable, the Clarendon Press, Messrs. Longmans, Messrs. Macmillan, the Oxford University Press, Messrs. Thornton Butterworth, and the Manchester University Press. Similar acknowledgments are also due to the Editor of *History*, the Historical Association, and the Editor of the *English Historical Review*.

CONTENTS

vii

CONTENTS

TO

CLARE AND N. H. B.

WHO KNOW WHAT IT MEANS

INTRODUCTION

AT the opening of the twentieth century there was some likeness between historians and the sons of contemporary business men. Just as the latter were inheriting complex organizations brought to a high pitch of efficiency and ready for unlimited expansion, so the successors to a group of distinguished historians were put in possession of rich resources and a wide field wherein to work. Their immediate predecessors had been active. They had raised the writing of history to a position of eminence among the literary arts, and had made it an indispensable part of the studies equipping men for membership of the cultured society of the day. They had enlarged its scope, improved its technique, discovered fresh stores of original materials their combined efforts did little more than reveal, and certainly did not come anywhere near exhausting. Still more important, however, was their success in combining their own studies with contemporary philosophical and political interests, so that the general reader, convinced of the importance of a knowledge of the past, was in sympathy with those whose labours were devoted to the writing of history.

These were advantages for the men entering into their heritage : but just as the heirs of business were soon to meet unexpected problems in a

changing world, so the historians were to find
some of their assets turn into liabilities. They
were not free men. Their route had been, in
some measure, mapped out by those who had
gone before them. It seemed as if they must for
ever be guided by the echoes of voices that were
stilled. True, there were many things for them
to do. They might be expected to add refinements
to technique already invented. They could, assuredly, dig more deeply into those yielding mines
of unpublished materials their masters had only
begun to exploit. There was a chance for them
to put finishing touches, here and there, to enterprises their predecessors had planned, and almost
brought to completion. So much was clear, and
if the scholars of the twentieth century had done
these things and nothing more, they would yet
have achieved much, for the nineteenth century
historians had not in any way completed the
enterprises they had dreamed. They deserve,
however, the credit due to those who refuse to be
mere imitators. The most superficial estimate of
their achievements must recognize work that was
planned on original lines. It could not have been
otherwise. Even if they had wished it they could
not have remained where they began, for a set
of swiftly changing circumstances forced them
to modify their ideas and compelled them to
be independent. Great advances in science
influenced their opinions. They met some unexpected developments—kaleidoscopic changes in
politics, materialist tendencies of thought, the
destruction of world order in a world war, the
speeding-up of the printing press, the spread of

a veneer of culture over masses previously untouched, the vulgarization of standards affected by the cinema and the daily press. These and influences of the same kind forced new problems upon them, and they were driven to go their own ways. They were roused from Victorian complacency by uneasy questionings about what they were doing. Were all the accepted maxims of the previous generation still true for their strange, new world ? The best among them were uncertain. They began to wonder if they really knew the nature and the purpose of the studies on which they were engaged. After all, what was History ? What were the functions of the Historian ? To such questions the nineteenth-century masters had given their answers, but their sons were not so sure those answers were correct. They had better find out for themselves, so not a few of the general discussions of the twentieth century have been concerned with these fundamental questions. In this book a great part of the available space has been given up to passages revealing some of the cross-currents of opinion on these matters, since the judgments the historian passes upon them provide a sure clue to the kind of history he will write.

The profound conviction with which Lord Acton stated his beliefs on these questions might well be taken as typical of the century that was gone, and the starting point for a study of opinion after his day. His was an omniscient scholarship, and the example of his learning, the ardour of his beliefs, exerted an influence on his contemporaries out of all proportion to the relative paucity of his written words. For Acton there was no question about the place historical studies must hold in modern society. The gift of historical thinking was for him more important than historical learning, and it was the supreme justification for time spent in gaining a knowledge of past events. His views on the function of the historian were equally clear-cut. From that ripe knowledge, the historian's reward for his labours, comes a deep reserve of strength and a steadying influence that is his unique contribution to modern life. Or, as Acton himself phrased it : " The knowledge of the past, the record of truths revealed by experience, is eminently practical, is an instrument of action, and a power that goes to the making of the future." Acton's standards for those undertaking such work were rigorous to a degree that failed to win the approval of many of his contemporaries, and in a measure they have been rejected by writers of the present generation. His influence, nevertheless, has been a powerful stimulus, and a survey of the tendencies of modern historical thought would be incomplete if it were left out of account.

Some of Acton's successors have gone further than he would have done in their conception of the nature of history. Early in this century there could be heard the note of challenge to established conventions of historical thought. It was heard at its clearest in the inaugural lecture delivered at Cambridge by Acton's successor in 1904. "History," said Bury in a sentence so often repeated that it has become commonplace, " is a science : nothing more, nothing less." Here, indeed, was an idea likely to cause much controversy, the inspiration for some novel ideas.

Bury's challenge suffered the fate of most epigrams. It was misunderstood. For our purpose, that is of more immediate importance than are the implications of the original statement, since the misunderstanding has had some very real effects upon the writing of history. The first effect we shall notice was the direct encouragement it gave to a movement, already in progress, for the application of the methods of science to the study of history. During the late nineteenth century the scientists had been developing very clear opinions as to what constituted scientific method, and these ideas, already known and to some extent used by historians, were now stressed more than ever under the authority of Bury's assertion.

Let us be clear : this was not in itself an evil. After all, the primary task of the historian, like that of the scientist, must always be the collection of facts. For that, each needs the same qualities. By each the collection of facts ought to be pursued with precision, with an alertness that detects the unusual and sees a problem in the commonplace. Each needs the same catholicity that allows absolute impartiality in the collection, and accuracy in the tabulation, of results. For each, too, the collection of facts is but the prelude to their classification ; for it is only by this second process that correlations will be discovered and a meaning be given to the collection. For such work historian and scientist alike need the discipline of the scientific method. It is this that enables each to let play upon his collected and classified facts the controlled imagination wherein lies the creative element each brings to his task. For each the imaginative process must be ordered by a cautious approach to problems, an agnosticism that shakes the head at judgments based on incomplete data, refuses to be led away by plausible but slipshod conclusions, and is on its guard against explanations tempting by reason of their simplicity or tidiness. All these principles of the scientific method apply just as forcibly to the historian as to the scientist, and in the discussions aroused by Bury's dictum both those who have approved and those who have rejected his conclusion have had no doubts that here they stand on common ground. Scientific method, however, is not science.

It would be foolish to deny that the principles of scientific method have conferred many benefits on the study of history. Insistence upon them has resulted in more rigorous standards of accuracy, greater emphasis on the necessity for the use of original materials, the invention of new methods for exploiting the available sources, and finally, a presentation of results that avoids prejudice without sacrificing the right to opinions. All this has been sheer gain. No amount of praise, however, can conceal the evils that the scientific method has brought in its train. As will be seen from some of the passages in this book, there have not been lacking critics whose opinion it is that the losses have been greater than the gains. There is reason in the criticism. As so often happens, enthusiasts have betrayed the cause by exploiting the scientific method beyond the point at which it becomes caricature and common sense yields place to the ridiculous. One is tempted to think that elaboration of the scientific method has brought into play the law of diminishing returns, with the result that the greater the emphasis on method, the less the amount of history written. While the number of historical monographs has grown steadily larger, the periods covered in each has become correspondingly shorter, and the problems studied have grown abstrusely technical. Further, these same tendencies have had other results that go deeper. The more specialized the problems studied, the greater has become the need for a technical vocabulary ; the more thorough the investigations, the greater the mass of details collected ; the more methodical the treatment and the more finished the technique, the more arid the finished product has become, and the less easy it is to find a way through the wood because of the trees.

Now, if these had been the only evil results of the use of the scientific method it would have been serious enough ; but there have been others. The worst was the outbreak amongst historians of a familiar epidemic. When scholars mutter abstractions—" man in the street," "the layman," " the general reader," and the like—they are beginning to feel that they are not as other men are, and cynical critics will diagnose intellectual snobbery. Of course, those historians who succumbed did not admit it. There was some rather stupid talk about the divorce of history from the general public, but the idea was usually wrapped up in more sententious language, to the effect that history was no longer a narrative of past events, but a science searching for universal laws, and as such could have little appeal for " the man in the street." Its results were technical; they need not be presented in literary form, for the historian was a scientist not an artist in words. In a word, history was a craft that was a mystery, and only the initiated could hope to master its secrets. It was against such opinions that Trevelyan tilted a lance in 1913, and in the years preceding the war there was much discussion of the problem whether history was or was not a science.

Now, the questions behind that controversy cannot be dismissed as cavalierly as men have sometimes presumed. It is easy to prove the importance of the contributions that have been made, and will continue to be made, by those engaged in the study of periods and problems necessarily academic in interest and technical in form. The results of such studies can often be best expressed in ways varying from a statistical table to an index, and in any discussion this fact must be faced. Those who wish to know the results of such work must be prepared to concentrate, for history, like every other study, imposes a discipline on those who read no less than on those who write. At the same time, it is fair to recognize that this non-literary type of historical work is not as important as is sometimes asserted. Much writing that repels by its pseudo-scientific jargon and lack of form is unnecessary, and is more often than not the result of slipshod thinking, and inexcusable laziness of mind. Even the most abstruse historical problems can and ought to be stated in language that will make them intelligible, even though they may not, by their very nature, be such as to make a widespread appeal. In short, the claim that history is a science, even if proved, does not relieve the historian from the obligation of making himself understood.

There are signs that this dispute about the relations of history to science and literature no longer interests historians. The excesses of the " scientific " historians have aroused much criticism, and historians find little profit in the old controversy. To-day there is among historians a keen recognition of their responsibilities to society, and they are anxious to make their influence felt as widely as possible by making the results of their work available to as large and interested a public as they can reach. Thus the arguments to-day all seem to be running in the direction of a truce. The best historical minds are concentrating attention on methods for making the most of all that has been achieved. Not for a moment would they think of giving up what has been won by the use of scientific method ; but on the other hand they still cling to the literary tradition. This is their dilemma. Can they continue to use the narrative form to express the scientific niceties of their discoveries ? The question has not as yet been adequately answered ; but the mere fact that it is being asked is a measure of the advance that has been made since the early years of the century, when the "science or art " controversy was at its height.

This welcome respite from the old discussions has been encouraged by other factors. Just as the idea of history as a science suffered from the follies of extremists, so, too, the idea of history as literature has had results that were not anticipated, and would certainly not be approved, by some of the leaders of the opposition to history as a science. If the results were deplorable when every historical worker fancied himself a scientist, what shall be said of the consequences when every trafficker in words sets up to purvey literary history? For this is what happened when the historians became superior persons, and isolated themselves from the general public. Even in the years before the war a popular demand for their services was becoming more insistent—through the wide spread of education, the progress of the public library movement, and the winning of leisure by large numbers of the community to whom it was a new privilege. Thus was created a growing public for which the novel was not the end of literature. The years following the war saw its numbers increase very rapidly. War, and its aftermath, created problems that—by reason of their novelty —threw men back upon the past in search of what they thought might help them in their troubles. They went inspired by a diversity of hopes. Some thought to find there information that would solve their problems, or warnings that would make them wise before events. Some went in search of hope, or dreamed of winning back the confidence in self and in humanity that they had lost. Some dared to seek ideals. Some merely hoped to find relief. Whatever motives prompted them, they sought their realization in a knowledge of the past. It was unfortunate that just when the historian was most in demand he was least in evidence. The result was inescapable. It was Mr. H. G. Wells.

Mr. Wells went to the past to look for the future, and he found it. That is what made his venture in universal history so popular with a generation that had gone to the past and found nothing, not even historians. As always, Mr. Wells gave the public what he thought it ought to want. This time it was a story as easy to read as a newspaper, as easy to buy—in instalments—as anything else on the railway bookstall, as full of pictures as a magazine, and as widely advertised as a star cinema film. That there was nothing very new in the idea of writing a history of the world—men had been writing them since the Middle Ages—was known only to those for whom this particular work did not cater, and even they were ready to admit that this was world history with a difference. Whether they liked it or not would make no effect on its phenomenal success. The Time Machine had arrived. Among the thousands and thousands who were hustled up and down the ages in it, there must have been many who came back dishevelled, their heads in a whirl, and their notions of whom and what they had seen decidedly vague. It must have been a staggering surprise to many to find God looking so much like the League of Nations, and not all of them could have suspected that Heaven was organized on Socialist principles. Nevertheless they had seen the sights. Or as they themselves would have said, so far as they were concerned Mr. Wells had " put history on the map." Thus was born the " new history," and its success encouraged imitators who were not as good, but who tried to go one better. Soon the writings of that group of artists in the best sense of the word—the advocates of the literary functions of the historians—were being parodied by vulgar cheap-jacks, who thought they were the equals of their betters when they imitated the fashions of these artists, but in fustian instead of silk. The stock-in-trade of these vulgarians has been monotonously uniform. It consists, in the main, of the following ingredients : a flamboyant style decked with cinema captions, an impudent self-assurance that passes uncritical judgments on the characters and problems of history, a nasty imagination which sees in the best of lives and the noblest of motives some pretext for " de-bunking " their victims, a crude smattering of psycho-analytic jargon used to introduce sensational revelations of sex motive, a thoroughly dishonest pretence of familiarity with original sources, and a complete irresponsibility in borrowing without recognition—or at best with a patronizing, half-concealed note of indebtedness in the preface—from the works of scholars whose labours provide the materials they misunderstand and misuse. There is no need to particularize this type of writing. It dies young. We may yet be grateful to it if it rouses the historian to a sense of his responsibilities. So far, he has not, on the whole, worried himself unduly about it. Indeed, that is probably all to the good. If he wastes time in reviewing it, he will be bound to say that what history it does contain comes from his own books or those of his colleagues, and then he lays himself open to a charge of petty jealousy. So he prefers to ignore it, and then he is criticized for being a superior person. There are bigger questions about the nature of history that interest the historians at present, and it is to some of these that we must now turn.

Obviously, the claim that history is a science means more than is implied by scientific method. It raises history to the dignity of a causal process, and allows for the formulation of universal laws. It would be impossible to consider within the limits of this essay all that is implied in such a claim. Better to take for granted the invigorating influences, in order to stress the dangers that come from uncritical use of analogies drawn from the natural sciences. This is the cause of disquiet to many historians. Here, again, what has aroused most alarm has been the absurdly exaggerated conclusions arrived at by those who have allowed enthusiasm to do the work of reason. Ignoring the obvious differences between the materials at the disposal of the historian and the scientist respectively, they have tried to make historical study perform the impossible, and thus have brought even the more acceptable elements in their theories into disrepute. The search for general laws governing human affairs has resulted in many ambitious enterprises, has produced some stimulating books, but the temptation to do violence to the facts in an attempt to maintain a thesis has often proved irresistible, with harmful results for the cause such books were intended to serve. The present century has witnessed many attempts of this kind, in which theories of progress, laws of contingency, complicated schemes of cycles of human development, and the like, have been applied to reduce within the limits of a formula as much of the data of social life as is possible. Most serious in recent years has been the challenge from the sociologists. In their efforts to stake out a claim for a science of society they have sought to limit the scope and the functions of history, and if the extremists among them could have their way history would by now be the handmaid of sociology, relegated to the duty of collecting data for others to use. The full force of this challenge has hardly been met, and the issue will not be reached until sociology has been disciplined to a degree that is not yet apparent. Until the wide claims and sweeping generalizations made by some of its more reckless advocates have been tempered, its proper place amongst the sciences will not be established, and historians must continue to doubt whether it has much to offer them. As is bound to be the case when such questions come up for discussion, benefit can be derived from an interchange of ideas, and historians will not be slow to adapt to their own purposes the more constructive suggestions the new school of thought may produce. For the moment that is as far as the matter can go.

In all these discussions there has so far been much activity, but no approach to finality. At the end of this period, as at the beginning, historians are content to hold different opinions on the scope of their work, as may be seen from the selections in the first part of this book. That the gulf between them can be wide is suggested by the last two passages. In 1935, while Professor Toynbee was devoting some six or more large volumes to a synthesis of human history built around fundamental principles, Dr. Fisher was surveying the wide field of Western history, and was regretfully coming to the conclusion that one intellectual excitement had been denied him. He could see in history no plot, rhythm, or predetermined pattern, but only the play, in the development of human destinies, of the contingent and the unforeseen.

.   .   .   .

In sketching the relations of the historian to the general public since 1900, something has been said to explain why the former retired into seclusion. It was, as we have seen, partly because of his changing views on the nature of history and of his own functions; but there have been other reasons, best summed-up as the ever widening scope of history. With the growing popularity of historical studies at the turn of the century came a great increase in the supply of historical workers and a phenomenal rise in the number of monographs, articles, and editions of original materials published. These added enormously to knowledge over the whole field of history; but every specialist soon found that it was almost more than he could do to keep abreast of the output in his own field. Few liked to undertake the task of going outside these narrow limits to put the results of recent investigations into language the plain man could understand. How was such work to be done? What plan could be devised to keep scholarship within the range of the general public ?

Largely through the inspiration of Lord Acton a way was devised. The work was to be shared out to specialists under the leadership of general editors. The latter were to be responsible for the general plan, the former were asked to write popular but scholarly accounts of limited periods, in which they were to incorporate the main results of the latest research. Thus was created *The Cambridge Modern History*, parent of a whole family of " syndicate " or " co-operative " histories.

Can the " syndicate " history be adjudged a success ? It is impossible to give an unqualified answer. Historians are divided in their opinions, but the individual most likely to be critical is that general reader for whom it was originally planned. It was intended to provide him with a simple exposition, in non-technical language, of recent specialist views ; and if—on the whole—it can be said to have done this, the scale on which it has been planned and the standard of knowledge it has to assume in its readers makes demands that are far too heavy. It is not surprising to find that the layman has come to look upon these histories as reference works wherein much admirable scholarship lies buried, rather than as specimens of historical writing he may read for pleasure. Whatever their merits—and they are many— these efforts in co-operative labour have not solved the problem set up by the estrangement of the historian from the man in the street. Meanwhile, that problem grows with the passing years, for the content of history goes on extending, and specialist and amateur alike find it more and more difficult to keep touch with all that is done.

If the scientists are right, we live in an expanding universe ; but what historians feel more acutely is that they are studying an expanding past. This is true, not merely in the sense that the present is forever becoming the past, but also by reason of the fact that improved technique enables the historian to stake out a larger claim on Time than was possible even a generation ago. This process is at work, if we may say so, at both ends of Time. The immediate past is nowadays appropriated more quickly as a sphere in which historians can and should work. Whereas Freeman's emphasis was that history is past politics, men of our day prefer to speak about politics as present history, or, in more academic language, give much emphasis to " contemporary " history. How far the desire for such an emphasis was quickened by post-war interests need not be discussed here, but in this selection there will be found some extracts that show how real is the enthusiasm aroused for such studies in many modern historians. Nor is this extension in time limited to the immediate past. It can be discerned also at the other end. The perfecting of historical method, the application of modern inventions like the aeroplane and the camera to the study of the past, the discoveries and the hypotheses of modern science, have all stimulated interest in the origins of man, so that much that used to be " pre-history " is no longer so, save in the sense that it is the past which has left no written evidence of its existence. Historical method has been applied to archæology with profound, yes revolutionary, results. So history has again on that side an ever-extending content in Time.

There is, too, the extension of knowledge that comes from ability to probe deeper, to make more use of what we know. That comes largely from a more finished technique in the handling of materials, although there has also been the discovery of new sources which have put us in possession of facts entirely unsuspected by historians of an earlier generation. Other factors have also made their contribution. Of these, not the least important have been the growth of special interests in modern society, which have posed new questions for historians to answer, and have suggested new interpretations of old knowledge. Illustrations of some of these new interests will be found among the selections in this book. These do not represent anything like all the developments that have taken place, but they will serve as a starting point for study of the question.

Brief as this introduction must be, it should be sufficient to hint at the variety and novelty of the problems the historians of the twentieth century have had to face. It would hardly be fair to expect from these men a full solution, or even an adequate policy, for dealing with such difficulties. These can only come from experiments, not all of which will be successful. Meanwhile, the failure to provide a solution has for the time being resulted in an estrangement between the specialist and the layman. There is, however, no reason to believe that this is likely to be permanent. The relation between historical knowledge and the life of modern society is too close to make it credible that the study of the past will ever be allowed to become the monopoly of a select coterie of pedants. And this means that layman and specialist must in the long run find, and maintain, contacts. Can they be made ? Can historians meet a popular demand ? We have seen that some of the methods proposed—the syndicate history and the untrained popularizer, for example— have failed. Is there any way whereby a reconciliation can be reached ? We may answer that question by asking another.

In all that has been said so far it has been assumed—critics always assume it—that modern historians have failed to make a popular appeal, that their works cannot be understood by readers not equipped with the requisite technical knowledge. Have we the right to make that sweeping assumption ? The third section of this book is intended to answer that question in the negative. Any one conversant with the amount and the quality of the history written in this country since 1900 will know that what is here put forward as representative is totally inadequate. Yet, with all its limitations, it will give the discerning reader an indication, even though it is incomplete, of the variety that has been so marked a characteristic of recent historical writing. From the specimens here collected it is possible to catch the historian in many moods. We can learn something from him when he is contemplating his materials or commenting on another's work in editing them.

We may get a valuable insight into the labours involved in his work when we read a preliminary essay designed to clear the ground for a study planned on a larger scale. There are more than a few hints here of the historical method in action —the search for facts, the criticism of accepted opinions, the tireless efforts to get near to the truth. These were the standards by which this selection was made. There was one test that was not used. These passages illustrating the historian at work were not singled out because they were specimens of fine writing. This is not an anthology of English prose style. For this essay will have gone very sadly astray if it has failed to make clear that the historians of recent years have not, in the main, regarded themselves as literary artists. There has been variety enough in the views they have held of the nature of history and the functions of the historian; but, one and all, they have their opinions, and these have affected their work. We have attempted to illustrate some of them. When all has been said, the question that remains to be answered about all of them is this : To what extent have they succeeded in combining advanced scientific research with an attractive presentation of its results ? It is a question that must be answered by the general reader.

Before he considers it, there is yet a word that needs to be addressed to him. While the historian has been to some extent to blame for the estrangement of these last years, it is a responsibility that is not entirely his. Some of the blame should surely pass to the layman whose grievances against historians can be reduced to one : that historical writing demands from its readers a measure of concentration. Is there any subject, be it science or art, concerned with any knowledge—from the principles of contract-bridge to the running of a motor car—that does not impose its discipline from those who read about it ? History cannot be the exception, unless it is to be looked upon as a mere story of things dead and gone, a story to be read as a means of passing an hour. This is not the motive that has animated true historical study. Whatever their opinions, all historians go to the past with questions for which they want answers. The problems that absorb their interest may vary in importance, but one and all they are real, and they cannot be understood without a conscious effort. All that readers have the right to demand from any writer is that he should be intelligible. It is for them to decide whether what he has to say is what they wish to know. If it is, they must be prepared to give, in order that they may receive. So the supreme test of all the historians represented in this book is that we have already stated : the skill each has shown in combining scientific work with clarity of exposition.

How do they stand such a test ? Without making extravagant claims, we may surely conclude that these representative historians of the early twentieth century have succeeded to a degree far beyond that which is usually allowed. Despite all the evil consequences of the historical method, there have been not a few able to free themselves from the restraints that have crippled their fellows. Among the passages in this selection will be found more than one treating of technicalities in English it is a distinction to have written and a pleasure to read. And that, needless to remark, is only another way of saying they have written what the plain man can understand. Ought an intelligent reader to ask for more ? If his yearning for a knowledge of the past is more than an affectation he will know what he wants and will not grudge the effort involved in obtaining it. There is the contribution that the layman is called upon to make to the study of history.

Meanwhile, the historian has his duty to perform. One of the most encouraging features of present-day historical study is the fact that the old controversies no longer appeal to historians. They now know that history cannot be classified in the rigid way adopted by earlier writers. There are encouraging signs that the new generation, in the light of that knowledge, is feeling its way towards a new exposition. When it comes, the writing of history will be all the richer for the discipline acquired from the scientific method historians will have learned to control, and history will once again be ready to take its place as one of the chief of the humanistic studies.

I

THE NATURE OF HISTORY

What are the qualities that make a historian ?
Obviously these three—a capacity for absorb-
ing facts, a capacity for stating them, and a
point of view.

 Lytton Strachey : *Portraits in Miniature.*

I

THE NATURE OF HISTORY

The Epoch of Full Grown History

IF the Past has been an obstacle and a burden, knowledge of the Past is the safest and surest emancipation. And the earnest search for it is one of the signs that distinguish the four centuries of which I speak from those that went before. The Middle Ages, which possessed good writers of contemporary narrative, were careless and impatient of older fact. They became content to be deceived, to live in a twilight of fiction, under clouds of false witness, inventing according to convenience, and glad to welcome the forger and the cheat. As time went on, the atmosphere of accredited mendacity thickened, until, in the Renaissance, the art of exposing falsehood dawned upon keen Italian minds. It was then that History as we understand it began to be understood, and the illustrious dynasty of scholars arose to whom we still look both for method and material. Unlike the dreaming prehistoric world, ours knows the need and the duty to make itself master of the earlier times, and to forfeit nothing of their wisdom or their warnings, and has devoted its best energy and treasure to the sovereign purpose of detecting error and vindicating entrusted truth.

In this epoch of full-grown history men have not acquiesced in the given conditions of their lives. Taking little for granted they have sought to know the ground they stand on, and the road they travel, and the reason why. Over them, therefore, the historian has obtained an increasing ascendency. The law of stability was overcome by the power of ideas, constantly varied and rapidly renewed ; ideas that give life and motion, that take wing and traverse seas and frontiers, making it futile to pursue the consecutive order of events in the seclusion of a separate nationality. They compel us to share the existence of societies wider than our own, to be familiar with distant and exotic types, to hold our march upon the loftier summits, along the central range, to live in the company of heroes, and saints and men of genius, that no single country could produce. We cannot afford wantonly to lose sight of great men and memorable lives, and are bound to store up objects for admiration as far as may be ; for the effect of implacable research is constantly to reduce their number. No intellectual exercise, for instance, can be more invigorating than to watch the working of the mind of Napoleon, the most entirely known as well as the ablest of historic men. In another sphere, it is the vision of a higher world to be intimate with the character of Fénelon, the cherished model of politicians, ecclesiastics, and men of letters, the witness against one century and precursor of another, the advocate of the poor against oppression, of liberty in an age of arbitrary power, of tolerance in an age of persecution, of the humane virtues among men accustomed to sacrifice them to authority, the man of whom one enemy says that his cleverness was enough to strike terror, and another, that genius poured in torrents from his eyes. For the minds that are greatest and best alone furnish the instructive examples. A man of ordinary proportion or inferior metal knows not how to think out the rounded circle of his thought, how to divest his will of its surroundings and to rise above the pressure of time and race and circumstance, to choose the star that guides his course, to correct, and test, and assay his convictions by the light within, and, with a resolute conscience and ideal courage, to remodel and reconstitute the character which birth and education gave him.

LORD ACTON, *Lectures on Modern History* (Inaugural Lecture, " On the Study of History "), pp. 4–6.

" New " History

MODERN History to-day, then, shall mean what might perhaps be called the New History, as distinct from the Old History. The New History is history written by those who believe that history is not a department of *belles-lettres* and just an elegant, instructive, and amusing narrative, but a branch of science. This science, like many other sciences, is largely the creation of the nineteenth century. It deals with the condition of masses of mankind living in a social state. It seeks to discover the laws that govern these conditions and bring about the changes we call Progress and Decay, and Development and Degeneracy—to understand the processes that gradually or suddenly make up and break up those political and economic agglomerations we call States—to find out the circumstances affecting the various tendencies that show their power at different times. Style and the needs of a popular audience have no more to do with history than with law or astronomy.

. . . .

History then, if I may sum up, is a science ; it must be worked on scientific methods, or it becomes worthless gossip. It is important to have in every nation students of history to supply true history ; not false history, therefore there must be facilities for such students at Universities and great libraries, and they must be employed by the State to work at the mass of materials that luckily exists for the study of national history. They must study and give us their results. We need not be afraid that their results will lack practical use. Such men will not be expensive : they only need the wages of going on : but among them there have been and there will be men whom England may be proud of. And now a practical suggestion or two, and this is where you come in. You must not starve research—it does not pay to do so ; you must help to build up great libraries for other ends than your own recreation, and great Universities for other ends than your own forwarding in life. You must buy books for them that few of you will ever want to read yourselves, and you must pay for the support of those people

whose work you will not be able yourselves
thoroughly to appreciate ; but all this will be
necessary to maintain the students that will be
digging out results for you, results that will in the
end profit you, often in some strange and unexpected way that you can hardly understand.
Most of you believe in democracy : if there is one
thing the study of history shows to be certain, it
is *that an ignorant democracy cannot last long*.

> F. YORK POWELL (" A General Survey of Modern
> History," printed in *Frederick York Powell*, by
> O. Elton, II., pp. 1 and 12).

A Challenge

IN the story of the nineteenth century, which has
witnessed such far-reaching changes in the geography of thought and in the apparatus of research,
no small nor isolated place belongs to the transformation and expansion of history. That transformation, however, is not yet complete. Its
principle is not yet universally or unreservedly
acknowledged. It is rejected in many places, or
ignored, or unrealized. Old envelopes still hang
tenaciously round the renovated figure, and
students of history are confused, embarrassed,
and diverted by her old traditions and associations. It has not yet become superfluous to insist
that history is a science, no less and no more ;
and some who admit it theoretically hesitate to
enforce the consequences which it involves.

. . . .

I may remind you that history is not a

branch of literature. The facts of history, like the facts of geology or astronomy, can supply material for literary art; for manifest reasons they lend themselves to artistic representation far more readily than those of the natural sciences; but to clothe the story of a human society in a literary dress is no more the part of a historian as a historian, than it is the part of an astronomer as an astronomer to present in an artistic shape the story of the stars. Take, for example, the greatest living historian. The reputation of Mommsen as a man of letters depends on his Roman History; but his greatness as a historian is to be sought far less in that dazzling work than in the *Corpus* and the *Staatsrecht* and the *Chronicles*.

> J. B. BURY, " The Science of History " (in *Selected Essays,* ed. H. Temperley, pp. 3, 9).

Four Questions

Now, there are three or four different kinds of questions which every student of history is called upon to answer, some of them elementary, some profound: there is the question when? and the question where? the question how? and the question why? The question when? is the most elementary and the least informing of all historical interrogations. That may sound strange to those who are in the habit of regarding history as mainly a matter of dates. But dates *per se* are almost useless; by themselves, they are merely mental lumber. It may be said that the knowledge of a

single accurate date has a certain educational
value deriving from its exactitude; and an extravagant importance is often attached to children's
knowing that the battle of Hastings was fought in
1066 and the battle of Waterloo in 1815. It may
be some corrective of this view, and some induce-
ment to temper justice with mercy in dealing with
infants ignorant of these details, if we remember
that, as a matter of sheer chronological fact, the
battle of Hastings was not fought in 1066, nor
that of Waterloo in 1815. For the Christian era
is at least four years out of the true reckoning, and
all events dated *anno domini* are to that extent
wrong. Numberless accepted dates are still more
erroneous. You may remember that elaborate
preparations were made in 1901 to celebrate the
thousandth anniversary of the death of Alfred the
Great; on the eve of the celebration a profound
but mischievous scholar, without any consideration
for the feelings of the organizers of this millenary
demonstration, proved that Alfred really died in
899 or 900 at the latest, and that the demonstrators
were two years after the fair.

The same uncertainty exists with regard to
nearly all dates before the Norman Conquest,
and a good many afterwards ; even so late as the
eleventh century the Anglo-Saxon Chronicle,
almost a contemporary authority, is some years
out in the date it assigns to Canute's visit to Rome.
So that whatever value attaches to the committing
to memory of these dates must be independent of
their scientific exactitude. Dates in fact are
valuable not in themselves but only in so far as
they enable us to determine the sequence of events,

for the sequences are an indispensable factor in ascertaining the causes of history. The mere repetition of dates without reference to their use and meaning involves a repellent waste of time and temper.

The question where? is really more important than the question when?; and it is a much more searching test of a student's understanding of history to inquire where the battle of Blenheim was fought, than when it was fought. Yet I am afraid that for every ten who could answer the second question, scarce one could be found to answer the first. And among the reforms to be effected in the methods of teaching history none is more urgent than a proper appreciation of historical geography, and a proper use of historical wall-maps.

The next question is that of how? and this is the subject of nearly all our histories. Few students have yet set themselves systematically to answer the most difficult and most profound of all historical questions, the question why? We take the things for granted, and are content with the outward manifestation, without troubling ourselves about the soul of things which causes those manifestations. Columbus, we know, discovered America in 1492 ; we accept that as a sufficient statement and proceed to treat it as the origin of New World history, and as one of the principal factors which differentiate the modern from the mediæval world. But why did Columbus discover America ? Why was America discovered towards the end of the fifteenth, and not at the end of the fourteenth or sixteenth centuries ? Why does modern, as distinct from mediæval, history begin where it does, and not at any other time ? This is the sort of problem we should try to solve ; compared with it, questions of when, where, and how are almost trivial. History can, perhaps, be little more than a story for children, but there is a time when sober students should put away childish things, or at least cease to regard them as a final object of intellectual effort.

Now, it is not possible to solve these problems completely. History is not an exact science. Nothing that is real and concrete can be exact. Mathematics are exact, but only because they deal with abstractions. Two may be equal to two in arithmetic, but they are generally unequal in real life ; no two men are exactly equal to two other men. The same may be predicted about other live and real things ; and there is no necessary correlation between two pence and two politicans, except the abstract numerical identity. There is always a gulf between the thing and the mathematical expression of it. By mathematics you can prove that Achilles, moving ten times faster than a tortoise, never overtakes it, if the tortoise has ten yards start ; for while Achilles does ten yards, the tortoise does one ; while Achilles does one, the tortoise does a tenth, and so on. And, however minutely you subdivide the distance between the two, you cannot get rid of it by mathematical means. But in real life Achilles disposes of the difficulty without much trouble. A line is said to be length without breadth, and Euclid does not say that this is absurd. But it is ; for a line without breadth cannot be seen, drawn, or imagined, and certainly never existed. The mathematical plane is unreal ; to reach it you must leave the realm of reality. When once you have risen to this exalted level, you may be as abstract, as absolute, and as exact as you please. But the truth that deals with concrete things is always relative ; absolute truth is an abstract ideal not attained in practical human affairs, and therefore not attainable in their history. History deals with an infinite number of variant facts, just as grammar does with an infinite number of variant uses ; generalizations deduced from these facts, like grammatical rules deduced from these uses, are all incomplete, and partially false ; there are exceptions to every rule.

— A. F. POLLARD, *Factors in Modern History*, pp. 33–36.

The Limitations of the Historian

HISTORY is not easy to define ; but to me it seems to mean the record of the life of societies of men, of the changes which those societies have gone through, of the ideas which have determined the actions of those societies, and of the material conditions which have helped or hindered their development. Nor is it only a branch of learning to be studied for its own sake, but a kind of know-ledge which is useful to men in daily life, " the end and scope of all history being," as Sir Walter Raleigh says, " to teach us by example of times past such wisdom as may guide our desires and actions." Therefore to know what was, and what came to pass, and why it came to pass, and to

44

represent both with fidelity for the instruction of later men, is the office of the historian. Here on the threshold arises the familiar dispute about the nature of the historian's task. Is history a science or an art ? Men give opposite answers according to their conception of the methods and the objects of the historian. One tells us that history is a science, nothing more and nothing less ; another that it is an art, and that one only succeeds in it by imagination. To me truth seems to lie between these two extremes. History is neither, but it partakes of the nature of both. A two-fold task lies before the historian. One half of his business is the discovery of the truth, and the other half its representation. And these are two tasks different in kind, and demanding very different qualities in the man who undertakes them.

The discovery of the truth is a scientific process. The historian finds out what the life of a given society was by means of the records it has left behind it. These records are of many kinds ; a cathedral and a castle, a picture and a monument, are just as much records as documents, and in some cases they are the only records we have. You will remember how Professor York Powell insisted on this point. In the main, however, the written or printed word is the kind of record upon which history must be based. To search for these records and to collect the evidence they supply is the first business of the historian. At the same time he has to weigh and to sift the materials he is collecting, to separate the true evidence from the false, and the trivial from the essential.

Now this first part of the historian's task is

purely scientific. The process by which he collects his facts and determines their value, is like the process by which the man of science gathers and weighs the results of his experiments and observations. As the materials with which these two deal differ in their nature their methods must differ in detail; nor can the historian obtain such exact and certain results as the man of science, but the spirit in which both conduct their investigations must be the same.

When he has discovered the truth the second part of the historian's task begins. He has to state the truth as it appears to him. He has to combine his facts, and to construct something out of them, either a description, or a story, or a demonstration. All his facts are equally true, but all are not equally important. He must select certain facts and bring them into prominence, and put other facts in the background, or even leave them out altogether as unimportant. He must show the connection of these facts with each other, and their causes and results. By this process of selection and arrangement he endeavours to reproduce the effect which the whole of the evidence has produced upon his mind. As we say familiarly " he puts his ideas upon paper "; that is, he strives to embody in some material form a conception of the past which is floating in his head. And this work of combination, construction, and re-creation is essentially artistic rather than scientific in its nature.

In each part of the historian's work he is brought face to face with its peculiar difficulties. When a man has familiarized himself with the evidence upon which the history of a particular period must be based, the difficulty of representing it comes home to him. How is he to compress into a small space a faithful representation of the life of the time, to represent the whole life in all its variety and complexity ? Suppose that, for a moment, the portion of the past he is studying seems to rise before him like a live thing with all its colour and all its movement, how is he to fix this fleeting vision upon paper and express it in words ? His canvas is too narrow, his tools are too imperfect ; and the more he strives, the more the limitations of his art are forced upon him. Shakespeare felt them when he complained of the difficulty of " turning the accomplishment of many years into an hour-glass " and presenting on the unworthy scaffold of the Globe events which " in their huge and proper life," filled "the vasty fields of France." Any man who seeks to represent human life through any medium feels it too.

In the scientific part of his task also, the historian must feel the difficulty of finding out the truth. If we go back to early times, the imperfect nature of the evidence is forced upon us at every moment. It is often a question of the interpretation of a single sentence or the trustworthiness of a single document. Even in dealing with better-known periods, such as the seventeenth century, the same difficulty arises. Often the really conclusive document is missing ; we know that something happened, but the piece of evidence which would explain why it happened, is non-existent, and the precise significance of the fact becomes a matter for inference or conjecture.

Sometimes a whole series of documents dealing with a particular episode has perished by accident or design, and shreds and patches of evidence must be collected from different sources to supply its absence.

As we approach our own day a new difficulty arises. If the historian of earlier times suffers from the paucity of his materials, the historian of modern times suffers from their superabundance. One life is too short to search through them. A mere catalogue of parliamentary reports fills a whole volume, and who shall number the volumes of Hansard ?

Everywhere, therefore, the historian is made conscious of the limitations of his own knowledge about the past, and the limitations of men's possible knowledge. He feels that he moves in a little circle of light, seeing as far as his little candle throws its beams ; and beyond that comes darkness. The wisest historians I have known recognized most fully how little they could know about the times they knew best, admitted the provisional nature of some of their conclusions, and were careful to distinguish between what was really certain and what was only probable.

Thus the historian is doubly limited ; first by the difficulty of finding out the facts, and then by the difficulty of representing them. Even if he seems for the moment to overcome both difficulties, how transitory and fragile is the reputation of histories that were welcomed as perfect in their day ! New documents are discovered, new facts come to light, accepted theories are overthrown. Nor is it only the details that are altered by fresh discoveries; the outline of the past seems to change as it grows more remote. The point of view is continually changing, and the relative importance of facts alters with it. For each age looks back upon the past from a different altitude, and with fresh eyes, demanding from him who tells the story the answer to new questions. It wants the history written over again to suit itself. So through this constant shifting of the perspective, as well as through the discovery of fresh evidence, standard histories grow imperceptibly obsolete, and become at last " alms for oblivion." Only those endure in which the matter is so solid and the form so perfect, and both so harmoniously united, that they still satisfy and charm, and seem to triumph over time. Only those endure in which the individuality of the writer is so impressed upon the book that it seems " to embalm and treasure up the precious life-blood of a master spirit," and becomes part of literature.

C. H. FIRTH, *A Plea for the Historical Teaching of History*, pp. 5–10.

The Muse of History

IT is necessary to ask, " What is history and what is its use ? " We must " gang o'er the fundamentals," as the old Scotch lady with the ear trumpet said so alarmingly to the new minister when he entered her room on his introductory visit. So I now ask, what is the object of the life of man *qua* historian ? Is it to know the past and enjoy it forever ? Or is it to do one's duty to one's neighbour and cause him also to know the past ? The answer to these theoretic questions must have practical effects on the teaching and learning, the writing and reading of history.

The root questions can be put in these terms : " Ought history to be merely the Accumulation of facts about the past ? Or ought it also to be the Interpretation of facts about the past ? Or, one step further, ought it to be not merely the Accumulation and Interpretation of facts, but also the Exposition of these facts and opinions *in their full emotional and intellectual value* to a wide public by the difficult art of literature ? "

The words in italics raise another question which can be put thus :

" Ought emotion to be excluded from history on the ground that history deals only with the science of cause and effect in human affairs ? "

It will be well to begin the discussion by considering the alleged " science of cause and effect in human affairs." This alleged " science " does not exist, and cannot ever exist in any degree of accuracy remotely deserving to be described by the word " science." The idea that the facts of history are of value as part of an exact science confined to specialists is due to a misapplication of the analogy of physical science. Physical science would still be of immense, though doubtless diminished value, even if the general public had no smattering thereof, even if Sir Robert Ball had never lectured, and Huxley had never slaughtered bishops for a Roman holiday.

The functions of physical science are mainly

two. Direct utility in practical fields ; and in more intellectual fields the deduction of laws of " cause and effect." Now history can perform neither of these functions.

In the first place it has no practical utility like physical science. No one can by a knowledge of history, however profound, invent the steam-engine, or light a town, or cure cancer, or make wheat grow near the arctic circle. For this reason there is not in the case of history, as there is in the case of physical science, any utilitarian value at all in the accumulation of knowledge by a small number of students, repositories of secrets unknown to the vulgar.

In the second place history cannot, like physical science, deduce causal laws of general application. All attempts have failed to discover laws of "cause and effect " which are certain to repeat themselves in the institutions and affairs of men. The law of gravitation may be scientifically proved because it is universal and simple. But the historical law that starvation brings on revolt is not proved ; indeed the opposite statement, that starvation leads to abject submission, is equally true in the light of past events. You cannot so completely isolate any historical event from its circumstances as to be able to deduce from it a law of general application. Only politicians adorning their speeches with historical arguments have this power ; and even they never agree. An historical event cannot be isolated from its circumstances, any more than the onion from its skins, because an event is itself nothing but a set of circumstances, none of which will ever recur.

To bring the matter to the test, what are the "laws" which historical "science" has discovered in the last forty years, since it cleared the laboratory of those wretched "literary historians?" Medea has successfully put the old man into the pot, but I fail to see the fine youth whom she promised us.

Not only can no causal laws of universal application be discovered in so complex a subject, but the interpretation of the cause and effect of any one particular event cannot rightly be called "scientific." The collection of facts, the weighing of evidence as to what events happened, are in some sense scientific; but not so the discovery of the causes and effects of those events. In dealing even with an affair of which the facts are so comparatively well known as those of the French Revolution, it is impossible accurately to examine the psychology of twenty-five million different persons, of whom—except a few hundreds or thousands—the lives and motives are buried in the black night of the utterly forgotten. No one, therefore, can ever give a complete or wholly true account of the causes of the French Revolution. But several imperfect readings of history are better than none at all; and he will give the best interpretation who, having discovered and weighed all the important evidence obtainable, has the largest grasp of intellect, the warmest human sympathy, the highest imaginative powers. Carlyle, at least in his greatest work, fulfilled the last two conditions, and therefore his psychology of the mob in the days of mob rule, his flame-picture of what was in very fact a conflagration, his portraits of individual characters—Louis, Sièyes, Danton, Marat, Robespierre—are in the most important sense more true than the cold analysis of the same events and the conventional summings up of the same persons by scientific historians who, with more knowledge of facts, have less understanding of Man. It was not till later in his life that Carlyle went mad with Hero-worship and ceased to understand his fellow-men with that all-embracing tolerance and sympathy which is the spiritual hall-mark of his *French Revolution.*

The weakness of that great book is that its author knew nothing in detail about the *ancien régime* and the " Old French Form of Life " that was destroyed. He described the course of the fire, but he knew nothing of the combustibles or of the match.

How indeed could history be a " science " ? You can dissect the body of a man, and argue thence the general structure of the bodies of other men. But you cannot dissect a mind ; and if you could, you could not argue thence about other minds. You can know nothing scientifically of the twenty million minds of a nation. The few facts we know may or may not be typical of the rest. Therefore, in the most important part of its business, history is not a scientific deduction, but an imaginative guess at the most likely generalizations.

History is only in part a matter of " fact." Collect the " facts " of the French Revolution ! You must go down to Hell and up to Heaven to fetch them. The pride of the physical scientist is attacked, and often justly. But what is his pride compared with the pride of the historian who thinks that his collection of " facts " will suffice for a scientific study of cause and effect in human affairs ? " The economist," said Professor Marshall, " needs imagination above all to put him on the track of those causes of events which are remote or lie below the surface." Now if, as Professor Marshall tells us, imagination is necessary for the economist, by how much more is it necessary for the historian, if he wishes to discover the causes of man's action, not merely as a bread-winning individual, but in all his myriad capacities of passion and of thought ! The man who is himself devoid of emotion or enthusiasm can seldom credit, and can never understand, the emotions of others, which have none the less played a principal part in cause and effect. Therefore, even if history were a science of cause and effect, that would be a reason not for excluding but for including emotion as part of the historian's method.

It was no unemotional historian, but the author of *Sartor Resartus*, who found out that Cromwell was not a hypocrite. Carlyle did not arrive at this result by a strictly deductive process, but it was none the less true, and, unlike many historical discoveries, it was of great value. Carlyle, indeed, sometimes neglected the accumulation of facts and the proper sifting of evidence. He is not to be imitated as a model historian, but he should be read and considered by all historical students, because of his imaginative and narrative qualities. While he lacks what modern historical method

54

has acquired, he possesses in the fullest degree what it has lost.

Carlyle uses constantly an historical method which Gibbon and Maitland use sometimes, and other historians scarcely at all—humour. The "dignity of history," whether literary or scientific, is too often afraid of contact with the comic spirit. Yet there are historical situations, just as there are domestic and social situations, which can only be treated usefully or even truthfully by seeing the fun of them. How else could Anacharsis Clootz' deputation of the Human Species to the French Assembly be profitably told ? " From bench and gallery comes ' repeated applause ' ; for what august Senator but is flattered even by the very shadow of the Human Species depending on him ? Anacharsis and the ' Foreigners' Committee ' shall have place at the Federation ; on condition of telling their respective Peoples what they see there. In the meantime, we invite them to the ' honours of the sitting, *honneur de la séance*.' A long-flowing Turk, for rejoinder, bows with Eastern solemnity, and utters articulate sounds ; but owing to his imperfect knowledge of the French dialect, his words are like spilt water ; the thought he had in him remains conjectural to this day."

I conclude, therefore, that the analogy of physical science has misled many historians during the last thirty years right away from the truth about their profession. There is no utilitarian value in knowledge of the past, and there is no way of scientifically deducing causal laws about the action of human beings in the mass. In short, the value of history is not scientific. Its true value is educational. It can educate the minds of men by causing them to reflect on the past.

Even if cause and effect could be discovered with accuracy, they still would not be the most interesting part of human affairs. It is not man's evolution but his attainment that is the great lesson of the past and the highest theme of history. The deeds themselves are more interesting than their causes and effects, and are fortunately ascertainable with much greater precision. "Scientific" treatment of the evidence (there only can we speak to some extent of "science") can establish with reasonable certainty that such and such events occurred, that one man did this and another said that. And the story of great events is itself of the highest value when it is properly treated by the intellect and the imagination of the historian. The feelings, speculations, and actions of the soldiers of Cromwell's army are interesting in themselves, not merely as part of a process of "cause and effect." Doubtless, through the long succeeding centuries the deeds of these men had their effect, as one amid the thousand confused waves that give the impulse to the world's ebb and flow. But how great or small their effect was, must be a matter of wide speculation ; and the ultimate success or failure, whatever that may have been, was largely ruled by incalculable chance. It is the business of the historian to generalize and to guess as to cause and effect, but he should do it modestly and not call it "science," and he should not regard it as his first duty, which is to tell the story. For, irrespective of " cause and effect," we want to know the thoughts and deeds of Cromwell's soldiers, as one of the higher products and achievements of the human race, a thing never to be repeated, that once took shape and was. And so, too, with Charles and his Cavaliers, we want to know what they were like and what they did, for neither will they ever come again. On the whole, we have been faithfully served in this matter by Carlyle, Gardiner, and Professor Firth.

It is the tale of the thing done, even more than its causes and effects, which trains the political judgment by widening the range of sympathy and deepening the approval and disapproval of conscience ; that stimulates by example youth to aspire and age to endure ; that enables us by the light of what men once have been, to see the thing we are, and dimly to descry the form of what we should be. " Is not Man's history and Men's history a perpetual evangel ? "

It is because the historians of to-day were trained by the Germanizing hierarchy to regard history not as an " evangel " or even as a " story," but as a " science," that they have so much neglected what is after all the principal craft of the historian—the art of narrative. It is in narrative that modern historical writing is weakest, and to my thinking it is a very serious weakness— spinal, in fact. Some writers would seem never to have studied the art of telling a story. There is no " flow " in their events, which stand like ponds instead of running like streams. Yet history is, in its unchangeable essence, " a tale." Round the story, as flesh and blood round the bone, should be gathered many different things—character drawing, study of social and intellectual movements, speculations as to probable causes and effects, and whatever else the historian can bring to illuminate the past. But the art of history remains always the art of narrative. That is the bed rock.

It is possible that, in the days of Carlyle and Macaulay, Motley and Michelet, too much thought was given to narrative, at least in comparison with other aspects of history, for absolutely too much can never be given. It is possible that when Professor Seeley said, " Break the drowsy spell of narrative. Ask yourself questions, set yourself problems," he may have been serving his generation. But it is time now for a swing of the pendulum. " The drowsy spell of narrative " has been broken with a vengeance. Readers find little " spell " in historical narrative nowadays—however it may be with the "drowsiness." . . . In this vexed question whether history is an art or a science, let us call it both or call it neither. For it has an element of both. It is not in guessing at historical " cause and effect " that science comes in ; but in collecting and weighing evidence as to facts, something of the scientific spirit is required for an historian, just as it is for a detective or a politician.

To my mind there are three distinct functions of history, that we may call the *scientific*, the *imaginative* or *speculative*, and the *literary*. First comes what we may call the *scientific*, if we confine the word to this narrow but vital function, the day-labour that every historian must well and truly perform, if he is to be a serious member of his profession—the accumulation of facts and the sifting of evidence. " Every great historian has been his own Dry-as-dust," said Stubbs, and quoted Carlyle as the example. Then comes the *imaginative* or *speculative*, when he plays with the facts that he has gathered, selects and classifies them, and makes his guesses and generalizations. And last but not least comes the literary function, the exposition of the results of science and imagination in a form that will attract and educate our fellow-countrymen. For this last process I use the word literature, because I wish to lay greater stress than modern historians are willing to do, both on the difficulty and also on the importance of planning and writing a powerful narrative of historical events. Arrangement, composition, and style are not as easily acquired as the art of type-writing. Literature never helps any man at his task until, to obtain her services, he is willing to be her faithful apprentice. Writing is not, therefore, a secondary but one of the primary tasks of the historian.

Another reason why I prefer to use the word " literature " for the expository side of the historian's work, is that literature itself is in our day impoverished by these attempts to cut it off from scholarship and serious thought. It would be disastrous if the reading public came to think of literature not as a grave matron, but as a mere *fille de joie*. Until near the end of the nineteenth century, literature was held to mean not only plays, novels, and *belles-lettres*, but all writing that rose above a certain standard of excellence. Novels, if they are bad enough, are not literature. Pamphlets, if they are good enough, are literature—for example, the pamphlets of Milton, Swift, and Burke. Huxley's essays and Maine's treatises are literature. Even Maitland's expositions of mediæval law are literature. Maitland, indeed, wrote well rather by force of genius, by natural brilliancy, than by any great attention paid to composition, form and style. But for us little people it is just that conscious attention to book-planning, composition, and style that I would advocate.

All students who may some day write history, and in any case will be judges of what is written, should be encouraged to make a critical study of past masters of English historical literature. Yet there were many places a little time ago where it was tacitly accepted as passable and even praiseworthy in an historical student to know nothing of the great English historians prior to Stubbs. And, for all I know, there are such places still.

.   .   .   .

The idea that histories which are delightful to read must be the work of superficial temperaments, and that a crabbed style betokens a deep thinker or conscientious worker, is the reverse of the truth. What is easy to read has been difficult to write. The labour of writing and rewriting, correcting and recorrecting, is the due exacted by every good book from its author, even if he know from the beginning exactly what he wants to say. A limpid style is invariably the result of hard labour, and the easily flowing connection of sentence with sentence and paragraph with paragraph has always been won by the sweat of the brow.

Now in the case of history, all this artistic work is superimposed on the labours of scholarship, themselves enough to fill a lifetime. The historical architect must quarry his own stones and build with his own hands. Division of labour is only possible in a limited degree. No wonder then that there have been so few historians really on a level with the opportunities of their great themes, and that, except Gibbon, every one of them is imperfect either in science or in art. The double task, hard as it is, we little people must shoulder as best we may, in the temporary absence of giants. And if the finest intellects of the rising generation can be made to realize how hard is the task of history, more of them will become historians.

Writing history well is no child's-play. The rounding of every sentence and of every paragraph has to be made consistent with a score of facts, some of them known only to the author, some of them perhaps discovered or remembered by him at the last moment to the entire destruction of some carefully erected artistic structure. In such cases there is an undoubted temptation to the artist to neglect such small, inconvenient pieces of truth. That, I think, is the one strong point in the scholar's outcry against " literary history " ; but if we wish to swim we must go into the water, and there is little use in cloistered virtue, nor much more in cloistered scholarship. In history, as it is now written, art is sacrificed to science ten times for every time that science is sacrificed to art.

. . . .

In the Victorian age the influence of historians and of historical thinkers did much to form the ideas of the new era, though less of course than the poets and novelists. To-day almost all that is characteristic in the mind of the young generation is derived from novelists and playwrights. It is natural and right that novelists and playwrights (provided we can count among them poets !) should do most to form the type of mind of any generation, but a little steadying from other influences like history might be a good leaven in modern gospels and movements.

The public has ceased to watch with any interest the appearance of historical works, good or bad. *The Cambridge Modern History* is indeed bought by the yard to decorate bookshelves, but it is regarded like the *Encyclopædia Britannica* as a work of reference ; its mere presence in the library is enough. Publishers, meanwhile, palm off on the public books manufactured for them in Grub Street—" publisher's books," which are neither literature nor first-hand scholarship. This is the type generically known as " Criminal Queens of History," spicy memoirs of dead courts and pseudo-biographical chatter about Napoleon and his family, how many eggs he ate and how many miles he drove a day. And Lady Hamilton is a great stand-by. The public understands that this kind of prurient journalism is history lightly served up for the general appetite, whereas serious history is a sacred thing pinnacled afar on frozen heights of science, not to be approached save after a long novitiate.

.   .   .   .

If, as we have so often been told with such glee, the days of " literary history " have gone never to return, the world is left the poorer. Self-congratulation on this head is but the mood of the shorn fox in the fable. History as literature has a function of its own, and we suffer to-day from its atrophy. Fine English prose, when devoted to the serious exposition of fact and argument, has a glory of its own, and the civilization that boasts only of creative fiction on one side and science on the other may be great but is not complete. Prose is seldom equal to poetry either in the fine manipulation of words or in emotional content, yet it can have great value in both those kinds, and when to these it adds the intellectual exactness of argument or narrative that poetry does not seek to rival, then is it sovereign in its own domain. To read sustained and magnificent historical narrative educates the mind and the character ; some even, whose natures, craving the definite, seldom respond to poetry, find in such writing the highest pleasure that they know. Unfortunately, historians of literary genius have never been plentiful, and we are told that there will never be any more. Certainly we shall have to wait for them, but let us also wish for them and work for them. If we confess that we lack something, and cease to make a merit of our chief defect, if we encourage the rising generation to work at the art of construction and narrative as a part of the historian's task, we may at once get a better level of historical writing, and our children may live to enjoy modern Gibbons, judicious Carlyles, and sceptical Macaulays.

G. M. TREVELYAN, " The Muse of History,"
in *The Recreations of an Historian*.

The Value of History

IT is not uncommon in our days of superficial impressionism and unstable convictions to doubt the value of history. As the past never repeats itself exactly in the same way as before, modern sceptics come to discard its memories as useless stories. And yet history, if studied without prejudice, teaches the greatest lesson of all—to treat social life not as a mechanical combination, but as an organic process. We are constantly striving to shape and improve it, but it cannot be pulled to pieces and resettled at pleasure, because its roots are in the past and its functions stretch over centuries. Its growth and defects have to be studied in the light of social biology, social hygiene, social pathology, not in that of social mechanics. This is why thoughtful men are instinctively or consciously attracted by the " links with the past " which are so numerous in our everyday existence.

P. VINOGRADOFF, *Collected Papers*, I., p. 222.

The Process of Growth

THOSE matters are fittest for history which exhibit a process of growth. The great periods of human history are not the long periods ; they are those times of change and crisis when the movements of humanity are quickened and made visible, when the stationary habits and conservative traditions of mankind are broken up, and one phase of civilization gives place to another, as the bud, long and slowly matured, suddenly bursts into flower. The story of the war in the air is a perfect example of this quickening process, whereby developments long secretly prepared, and delayed until hope is saddened, are mysteriously touched with life, and exhibit the tendencies of ages condensed in the events of a few crowded years. The flying machine, which at the end of the nineteenth century was a toy, ten years later was added to the most valuable resources of Man, and ten years later again bid fair to alter the conditions of his life on the surface of the earth. The war, though it did not cause this great change, accelerated it enormously. War is exacting, and it is difficult to think of any peaceful uses of aircraft which do not find their counterpart in naval and military operations.

.　　.　　.　　.　　.　　.　　.

As the uses of aircraft multiplied, so did their designs, and where many various tasks were performed, in the beginning of the war, by a single type of machine, good in its day, there are now many types of machine, each with special fitness for its own purpose. How far these developments may yet go, no man can tell, and prophecy is idle ; what is certain is that many operations of war and peace which have never yet been performed are within the reach of the aircraft that are now at our disposal. A beleaguered city could be victualled. A force of a thousand men, with rations and ammunition, could be landed, in a few hours, to operate in the rear of an invading army. But the world is tired of war, and the advances of the immediate future will rather be made in the direction of peaceful traffic and peaceful communication.

The history of the war in the air is the history of the rapid progress of an art and the great achievements of a service. In the nature of things the progress of the art must claim a share in the record. If the battle of Trafalgar had been fought only some ten short years after the great adventurer trusted himself to the sea on a crazy craft, the ships, rather than the men, would be the heroes of that battle, and Nelson himself would be overshadowed by the *Victory*. The men who fought the war in the air have overcome more than their enemies ; they, and those who worked for them on the ground, have successfully grappled with problem after problem to the perfecting of the art of flight. A whole world of scientific devices, from the Pitot tube, which indicates the speed of the machine through the air, to the Dreyer automatic oxygen apparatus, which enables the pilot to breathe in the rarified upper reaches of the atmosphere and to travel far above the summit of high mountain ranges, has become a part of daily usage. A machine is the embodiment of human thought, and if it sometimes seems to be almost alive, that is because it springs of live parents. The men of science, who worked for humanity, must have an honour only less than the honour paid to the men of action, who died for their country.

SIR WALTER RALEIGH, *The War in the Air*,
pp. 8–13.

WE know next to nothing of man's greatest achievements. His written history is the history of yesterday, and leaves him very much the same being as it finds him, with the same habits, the same prejudices, and only slightly enhanced powers. The greatest and most significant advances were prehistoric. What invention, of which any record remains, can compare in importance with the invention of Speech ; and what day in the world's history is more worthy of celebration than that day, the birthday of thought and truth, when a sound, uttered by the breath, from being the expression of a feeling became the mark of a thing ? The man who first embarked on the sea has been praised for the triple armour of his courage ; but he must be content with praise ; his biography will never be written. The North American Indians are reckoned a primitive people, but when first they come under the notice of history they bring with them one of the most perfect of human inventions—the birch-bark canoe. What centuries of dreams and struggles and rash adventures went to the inventing and perfecting of that frail boat ? What forgotten names deserve honour for the invention of the paddle and the sail ? The whole story is beyond recovery in the rapidly closing backward perspective of time. Man's eyes are set in his head so that he may go forward, and while he is healthy and alert he does not trouble to look behind him. If the beginnings of European civilization are rightly traced to certain tribes of amphibious dwellers on the coast of the Mediterranean, who reared the piles of their houses in the water, and so escaped the greater perils of the land, then some sort of rudimentary navigation was the first condition of human progress, and sea-power, which defies the devastators of continents, had earlier prophets than Admiral Mahan. But the memory of these thousands of years has passed like a watch in the night.

The conquest of the sea can never be recorded in history; even the conquest of the air, which was achieved within the lifetime of all but the very youngest of those who are now alive, admits of no sure or perfect record. The men who bore a part in it, and still survive, are preoccupied with the future, and are most of them impatient of their own past. Where knowledge begins, there begin also conflicting testimonies and competing claims. It is no part of the business of this history of the war in the air to compare these testimonies or to resolve these claims. To narrate how man learned to fly would demand a whole treatise, and the part of the history which ends in December 1903 is the most difficult and uncertain part of all. Yet the broad outlines of the process can be sketched and determined. It is a long story of legends and dreams, theories and fancies, all suddenly transformed into facts; a tale of the hopes of madmen suddenly recognized as reasonable ambitions. When in the light of the present we look back on the past our eyes are opened, and we see many things that were invisible to contemporaries. We are able, for the first time, to pay homage to the pioneers, who saw the promised kingdom, but did not enter it. No place has hitherto been found for their names in serious history.

SIR WALTER RALEIGH, *The War in the Air,*
pp. 15–16.

Problems

IDENTITY in difference and difference in identity might be described as two of the chief problems for the historian. It is easier to see the difference than the identity; but without a sense of the latter all study of history, whether political or social, is vain.

C. L. KINGSFORD, *Prejudice and Promise in Fifteenth Century England*, p. 29.

History and Human Nature

THERE is a school which maintains that an historian should set down all facts coldly and dispassionately. He must (they insist) employ his critical faculty rigidly and without mercy; he must apply the most searching tests to ascertain the veracity of every writer of every document; and the spirit that informs the whole of his work should be cold and scientific. The reader should never be able to divine from the text the status, profession, nationality—nor, presumably, the age or the sex—of the writer. Thus may history " draw ever closer to those sciences which deal objectively with the facts of nature." Anyone who has followed me thus far will, I think, smile

very quietly at such pretensions. The historian
has to do, no doubt, with the facts of nature, but
principally with the facts of human nature. A
document, I repeat, is a scrap of human nature,
or it is naught. The study of history is the study
of human nature, or it is naught. But the science
of human nature is a thing which the best human
brains have struggled for centuries to found in
vain.

. . . .

It may be lamentable, but I think it is certain,
that the great majority of people will not read any
story if it be dull. Now the rules of the scientific
school, in banning literary art, unquestionably
tend to make history dull. Indeed, there are some
who think that history is not to be taken seriously
unless it be dull ; that, if it be lively, it is unscientific ; and that, as a natural consequence, it
is scientific to be dull.

Now dullness is, of course, a relative term, and
what is dull to many is not dull to all. The tall
volumes of Calendars of States Papers, for example,
present rather a forbidding aspect, but there are
some of us who can read certain of them for hours
with intense enjoyment. The Venetian series and
the Domestic series of the sixteenth century are full
of good things, and alive with human nature in all
its aspects. . . . Now why should not the human
nature in these and the like documents be made a
pleasure to the reader by the help of literary art ?
There is no occasion to distort or falsify recorded
facts or to invent new ones. Good sound material
abounds for him who has the knowledge to interpret it, and the literary skill to make it acceptable.

70

We are told, and rightly told, that it is of the first importance to the nation and to the world that every citizen should study history and study it intelligently. Why, in the mistaken name of science, should we make the task unpleasing to him? It is by no means certain that by the scientific method we get any closer to the truth than by the literary method. Naked facts, whose very nakedness must often be questionable, may be so collocated as to produce, even with honest intent, a very false impression. And, even if the scientific method could be counted upon to arrive at the truth, why should the truth be made repellent? People are unwilling enough to face it in everyday life; why extend that unwillingness also to the past?

In fact, these scientific histories, constructed on the approved principles, may be theoretically perfect; but, if nobody reads them, their perfection is thrown away. They fall into the same category with Calendars of Patent Rolls. They are not so much history as material for a history. They will be neglected until some one assimilates them and reproduces them in a readable, which is to say a literary, form. This means that they must be filtered through yet one more mind of an infinite series; and thus some of their real worth must be lost. This is a pity, but it is inevitable. We must never forget that history is not only the record of human nature, but that it must be imparted to creatures of human nature. In the instruction of children wise mothers remember this. Which of them, when telling the story of Samuel, would omit the detail, " Moreover, his mother made him a little coat " ? And the ordinary adult equally clamours for such touches of human nature, otherwise he will not read history.

SIR JOHN FORTESCUE,
The Writing of History, pp. 28–29, 41–44.

The Poetry of History

THE appeal of History to us all is in the last analysis poetic. But the poetry of History does not consist of imagination roaming at large, but of imagination pursuing the fact and fastening upon it. That which compels the historian to " scorn delights and live laborious days " is the ardour of his own curiosity to know what really happend long ago in that land of mystery which we call the past. To peer into that magic mirror and see fresh figures there every day is a burning desire that consumes and satisfies him all his life, that carries him each morning, eager as a lover, to the library and muniment room. It haunts him like a passion of almost terrible potency, because it is poetic. The dead were and are not. Their place knows them no more and is ours to-day. Yet they were once as real as we, and we shall to-morrow be shadows like them. In men's first astonishment over that unchanging mystery lay the origins of poetry, philosophy, and religion. From it too is derived in more modern times this peculiar call of the spirit, the type of intellectual curiosity that we name the historical sense. Unlike most forms of imaginative life it cannot be satisfied save by facts. In the realm of History, the moment we have reason to think that we are being given fiction instead of fact, be the fiction ever so brilliant, our interest collapses like a pricked balloon. To hold our interest you must tell us something we believe to be true about the men who once walked the earth. It is the fact about the past that is poetic ; just because it really happened, it gathers round it all the inscrutable mystery of life and death and time. Let the science and research of the historian find the fact, and let his imagination and art make clear its significance.

G. M. TREVELYAN, *The Present Position of History*, p. 28.

The Missing Muse

FOR Clio, in spite of a gallant essay in her honour by Professor George Trevelyan, has vanished from the haunts of men—of English-speaking men, that is to say. For she left the Continent years ago after an unsuccessful attempt to learn German. The Muse of History, who once walked among us and leaned above bowed shoulders breathing style into learned pages and life into dead folios, has vanished; and while the incense steams on other altars and historians dash themselves before the Mumbo Jumbo of a vast card-index, the art of history has vanished with her. So we are left in the draughty ruins of her temple, lamenting the sad state of something that was once a great branch of English letters.

The art of history is, perhaps, an awkward term to use, if by calling history an art we mean to

73

deny its claim to be a science. For in a democratic age everything is a science, from the random anecdote of psycho-analysis to the uncorrelated data of economics. We are all, as Sir William Harcourt almost cried, scientists now. The tipster and the statistician, the thought-reader (now transferred from country fairs to Chairs of Psychology in universities) and his less articulate sister, the palmist, have each staked an indisputable claim to the dignity of scientists. The only pity is that most seances are left in the hands of total illiterates.

But history, at least, must not be of their number. For though history is a full-fledged science in the narrow sense that its sole foundation must be a body of scientifically ascertained facts, it is also something more. Few satisfactory edifices consist of a foundation alone. The facts, however scientific, require to be presented ; and in their presentation the historian is inevitably something more (or is it less ?) than a scientist. Bare tabulation will not do ; simple enumeration is plainly insufficient. There must be a hint of perspective. The historian must select, and in the awkward process of selection he becomes an artist. One seems to see him at this uncomfortable stage desert the laboratory and furtively approach the studio. And why not ? There is no need for him to blush when we detect him in the questionable company of artists. For history is an art as well— the art of representing past events through facts of scientific accuracy. If the facts are inaccurate, it is not history. But if they are not embodied in the picture of a living past, it is not history either.

For a smear on a palette is not a picture. So the historian, when his work among the test-tubes of research is done, must turn artist, discarding his overalls for the velvet jacket. If he cannot, so much the less historian he.

. . . . . .

Once, just ninety years ago, an historian of the most solemn purpose could avow that he meant " to splash down " what he knew of the French Terror " in large masses of colour that it may look like a smoke and flame conflagration in the distance." How strangely his confession reads to a generation whose average impression of any complex historical event, if it has learnt its lessons, is that it looked like an accident to a card-index. And yet the smoke, the hungry flame, the cries were not, one feels, wholly unlike the Terror. For Carlyle applied his imagination to the facts —an historian's imagination, which assembles scientific facts into a visible picture and is totally distinct from the pure invention of the novelist. " Imagination," as Sir John Fortescue once informed a startled audience of historians, " must not be construed as synonymous with invention. . . . It is rather *re*-creative and *re*-productive. It is the power of bringing back to the mind the impression that objects might give or have given. Obviously, therefore, the historian, whose business it is to re-create or interpret the past, must rely upon the only medium that is capable of producing that effect—imagination primarily, and not the generalizing intellect. Imagination is, therefore, not only invaluable, but essential to the historian." Once more, is it the dawn ? And do we hang upon the verge of an admission that the historian's duty is not merely to catalogue dry bones in a museum, but to make them live ? If so, how very few of them achieve it.

The field of history is, at the present time, a singularly depressing landscape. One almost sees it as a cheerless little garden, in which the biting north-easter out of Germany permits none but the hardiest flowers to bloom. Here Professor Trevelyan rears his gallant head ; there a shy blossom or so grows on the stony soil which Acton sprinkled liberally with the rocks of syndication. Indeed, the plants in poor Clio's border are mainly rock plants ; and we should deal tenderly with these shy apologies for flowers. How small they are ; how easily discouraged ; how chilled, when Croce damps them with the vast watering can of his *Theory and History of Historiography* ; how scared when Dr. Gooch stoops in his *History and Historians in the Nineteenth Century* to administer a pinch of weed-killer to a small bloom that thought it was a flower. Small wonder that the Muse is rarely seen walking in her garden.

What are the causes ? Primarily, one feels, the chill north-easter. It is still blowing hard across the North Sea (and even across the Atlantic) from the German flats. For British scholarship has worn the *Pickelhaube* for almost half a century now ; and in America, where Germany has always been the supreme finishing-school, the influence is still more undoubted. No Chauvinist would seek for an instant to deny the magnitude of the Anglo-American debt to German methods and inspiration. But, vastly the gainers by it, are we not also losers ? The conquest of our historical schools was almost too complete, the peace-treaty so manifestly one-sided ; and it is time, perhaps, for the wise adjustments of an historical Locarno. For whilst it is good for historians to be sent to the documents, was it altogether good for the documents to be presented in undigested masses without perspective and in the unsound belief, attributed by one malicious critic to a too scientific rival, that " all facts are born free and equal ? " It is time to recall that the document is a means, and not an end ; that the researcher's thread must find its place one day in the historian's tapestry ; that brick-makers are well enough, but that the edifice of history calls for an architect as well—an architect who, as Professor Trevelyan has written, " must quarry his own stones, and build with his own hands." The task is frightening. Small wonder that the weaker brethren prefer to pass a lifetime in the quarries. The risks are fewer, and the rewards of steady manual labour are respectable. But still the work is waiting . . .

PHILIP GUEDALLA,
The Missing Muse and Other Essays.

Philosophies of History

THE craving for an interpretation of history is so deep-rooted that, unless we have a constructive outlook over the past, we are drawn either to mysticism or to cynicism. A man who feels no sense of correspondence between his experience and the object of his study, and has no idea of

77

values proper to it, may become a dilettante, a lounger in the wake of philosophy or science. Philosophies of history have been more powerful than history, for, in one form or another, from the system of St. Augustine to those of Hegel and Karl Marx, they appeal to man's sense of destiny. Yet there can be no doubt that the study of history as history, and not as the instrument of a single conception or theory, has steadily undermined the influence of the philosophies of history, while it has given new force to what is enduring in them. Despite his great range of knowledge, I doubt if Spengler in the twentieth century will have as much influence as Joachim of Flora had in the thirteenth. History could not do this if it had no value of its own, if there were no correspondences which, in every age, are suggested by some dominating interest or need, but whose form is dictated by the material of history, not imposed upon it. Their form of expression changes with the growth of the knowledge which the interest in them brings about. To take a well-known example : interest in the problem of the regulation of trade by the state suggested that the economic history of England in the fourteenth and sixteenth century had peculiar significance ; the policy of Edward III. and of Elizabeth was studied, the history of their times made more coherent, and, so to speak, put into shape ; but the conclusions ultimately reached about Edward III. and the Merchant Adventurers were very different indeed from the first impressions—the shape changed. The material has a controlling interest in the expression of our sense

of correspondence although this latter itself
changes with our own needs and interests. When
Voltaire undertook to show that modern history
can be made as interesting as ancient history, he
was influenced by a strong belief in the value of
modern culture as a means of self-expression. His
ideal was civil and religious liberty in an ordered,
humane, polished world, and he studied the developments of history from this point of view. Its
value to him lay there. In the nineteenth century,
history was studied from the point of view of the
national state, and, within this conception, of
political liberty or political strength, as the case
might be. Hence the profound investigations
into the nature of law, the growth of political
forms, the types of statecraft, the development of
foreign policy. Modifying these interests was the
influence of geological and biological investigation, the influence which provoked York Powell's
epigram that Lyall and Darwin were the chief
modern historians. The study of history could
no longer be confined to a few kinds of human
activity, for the conventional framework of human
life had been shattered. The war seemed to
dislocate all our outlook on life. It has loosened
many old allegiances, while it has given an impetus
to the interest in history, and this at a time when
the marvellous development in the physical
sciences has brought still more fundamental
conceptions in question. Confidence in these is
shaken, while we are hesitating again about the
idea of sovereignty and the meaning of the state.
All kinds of interests, suggesting new values, are
playing upon or with history. Corresponding to

the romantic movement of a century ago, though
very different in its metallic certainties, is the
movement for which the Germans have already
found the name " historische Belletristik," the
application to history of psychological analysis in
a finished literary form. Many people, uncertain
of the old values and dispirited by an ever
accumulating mass of intractable material, find
something positive and interesting in this. But
the constructive impulse cannot be checked. The
sense of order, the faculty of judgment will assert
themselves. They are asserting themselves before
our eyes, and I believe that the immediate concerted attack upon the innumerable records of
world history since 1914 will be regarded in the
future as one of the finest achievements in historical scholarship. It would not have been
possible thirty years ago. The energy which can
face a task like this will not fail to express itself
elsewhere. For this expression of energy is part
of a general constructive idealism which gives
new meaning to history.

F. M. POWICKE, *Historical Study in Oxford*, pp. 15–17.

Changing Views of History

HISTORY has sometimes been invoked to demonstrate a belief in the progress of humanity, in the
truth of Christianity, or even in the existence of
God. All such attempts serve only to make
history the handmaid of science or of dogma or
of philosophy. History should be studied for
herself alone. The appeal history makes is both

intellectual and emotional, but it is limited and objective in its scope, and is becoming more so. In my own memory the idea that history is a science has perished, and the effects of this change of view are already evident. It was thought necessary only twenty years ago to demonstrate that impartiality was impossible in history. I remember hearing the late Archdeacon Cunningham read a paper to that effect. This great Cambridge figure—who drew arguments from medieval economics for modern polemical controversy—convinced by example even more than by argument. But the theory that an historian could be really impartial seems to us to-day one of manifest buckram. We wonder that any one troubled to destroy it. I suppose traditions of science or scientific impartiality still hung about history and that they have faded away as Clio advanced again into the foreground. If we look with the eyes of a literary artist we shall see at once why. " In making even horizontal and clear inspections," says Thomas Hardy, " we colour and mould, according to the wants within us, whatever our eyes bring in ! " * Historical inspections are not usually either horizontal or clear, so that colouring and moulding must needs be emphasized. We admit it now to the full. Not only do we repudiate the ideal of Ranke that history should be colourless, new, and impartial. We do not even suggest that it is desirable.

Not only is the method of colourless scientific impartiality discredited, but in one direction at least the literary method has extended. I think

* *Far from the Madding Crowd,* chap. ii.

that it is recognized in an increasing degree that the imaginative gifts of great writers can produce great results in the sphere of historical romance. There is a famous interview between Napolean and Balasov on the eve of the Russian campaign, which is more correctly described by Tolstoy, an avowed romancer working on a few fragments of knowledge, than by historians working on the amplest records. So long as the work is avowedly fiction.

.   .   .   .   .   .

At the same time that it was recognized that the historical world needed colour and life, methods of precision and not of pseudo-science were being applied to the advancement of knowledge. Progress has recently been made in modern historical research by limiting aims, by increasing objectivity, and by abandoning vain speculation. The results are already remarkable. As the shadow of impartiality fades its substance takes shape. Acton tells us that " knowledge has prevailed over opinion " ; Trevelyan, that " each year there is less ground for the perpetual misrepresentation employed by creed, class, and race." Here we have traces of authentic victories which have been won over stubborn foes and on stricken fields. They have been won over armies as innumerable as they were reported to be invincible ; and over mental stiles against which even the gods have hitherto fought in vain. The Anglo-Saxon race has sacrificed its patriotic ideals on the altar of truth. English-speaking historians have gradually destroyed the patriotic belief that our Saxon ancestors were democrats and that our parliament was a unique, or even a legislative, institution. American historians are slowly causing the American people to give up the belief that George III. was a tyrant and to admit that economic, as well as political, motives supplied fuel to the revolutionary ardour. These conversions of public opinion to common sense make us hope that one day history will prevail over public opinion. But it is not enough that England and America have begun to adjust their historical differences. Further victories remain to be won. We should work and work towards the age when France and Germany will do so. That end is certainly far. National history is not likely to cease to be written, international history in the true sense has hardly even begun. But I think that no historian will do wrong if he studies the stories of other countries besides his own and occasionally views our own history with the eyes of a foreigner.

HAROLD TEMPERLEY, *Research and Modern History*,
pp. 18–20.

A Confession

I BEGIN this book with neolithic man and conclude with Stalin and Mustapha Kemal, Mussolini, and Hitler. Between these rough and rugged frontiers there are to be found some prospects flattering to human pride which it is a pleasure to recall to memory, the life-giving inrush of the Aryan peoples, the flowering of Greek genius, the long Roman peace, the cleansing tide of Christian ethics, the slow reconquest of classical learning after the barbaric invasions, the discovery through oceanic travel of the new world, the rationalism of the eighteenth and the philanthropy and science of the nineteenth centuries. One intellectual excitement has, however, been denied me. Men wiser and more learned than I have discovered in history a plot, a rhythm, a predetermined pattern. These harmonies are concealed from me. I can see only one emergency following upon another as wave follows upon wave, only one great fact with respect to which, since it is unique, there can be no generalizations, only one safe rule for the historian : that he should recognize in the development of human destinies the play of the contingent and the unforeseen. This is not a doctrine of cynicism and despair. The fact of progress is written plain and large on the page of history ; but progress is not a law of nature. The ground gained by one generation may be lost by the next. The thoughts of men may flow into the channels which lead to disaster and barbarism.

H. A. L. Fisher, *A History of Europe*, I., vii.

II

THE WIDENING SCOPE OF HISTORY

History is the curse of modern education :
it not only doubles itself as time goes on, as
population increases, and as people segregate,
but not content with this, it burrows in the
past for new (and best forgotten) facts for
boys to be crammed with.
  Leonard Huxley : *Life and Letters of
    Sir Joseph Dalton Hooker*, II., 262.

II

THE WIDENING SCOPE OF HISTORY

The Need for Co-operation

SEVENTY - FIVE years have passed since Lingard completed his *History of England*, which ends with the Revolution of 1688. During that period historical study has made a great advance. Year after year the mass of materials for a new *History of England* has increased; new lights have been thrown on events and characters, and old errors have been corrected. Many notable works have been written on various periods of our history; some of them at such length as to appeal almost exclusively to professed historical students. It is believed that the time has come when the advance which has been made in the knowledge of English history as a whole should be laid before the public in a single work of fairly adequate size. Such a book should be founded on independent thought and research, but should at the same time be written with a full knowledge of the works of the best modern historians and with a desire to take advantage of their teaching wherever it appears sound.

The vast number of authorities, printed and in

manuscript, on which a History of England should be based, if it is to represent the existing state of knowledge, renders co-operation almost necessary and certainly advisable. The *History*, of which this volume is an instalment, is an attempt to set forth in a readable form the results at present attained by research. It will consist of twelve volumes by twelve different writers, each of them chosen as being specially capable of dealing with the period which he undertakes, and the editors, while leaving to each author as free a hand as possible, hope to insure a general similarity in method of treatment, so that the twelve volumes may in their contents, as well as in their outward appearance, form one *History*.

As its title imports, this *History* will primarily deal with politics, with the History of England and, after the date of the union with Scotland, Great Britain, as a state or body politic ; but as the life of a nation is complex, and its condition at any given time cannot be understood without taking into account the various forces acting upon it, notices of religious matters and of intellectual, social, and economic progress will also find place in these volumes. The footnotes will, so far as is possible, be confined to references to authorities, and references will not be appended to statements which appear to be matters of common knowledge and do not call for support. Each volume will have an Appendix giving some account of the chief authorities, original and secondary, which the author has used. This account will be compiled with a view of helping students rather than of making long lists of books without any notes as to their contents or value. That the *History* will have faults both of its own and such as will always in some measure attend co-operative work, must be expected, but no pains have been spared to make it, so far as may be, not wholly unworthy of the greatness of its subject.

Editor's Introduction to *The Political History of England.*

In Defence of the Syndicate History

IT is no longer possible for the historian of modern times to content himself with a picturesque presentation of outward events. In fact, however much he may try to limit the ground which he intends to occupy, he finds himself drawn insensibly into a larger sphere. His subject reveals unsuspected relations with problems which afterwards became important. He perceives tendencies to have been at work which helped to produce definite results under the unforeseen conditions of a later age. He discovers illustrations, all the more valuable because they represent an unconscious process, of forces destined to become powerful. His work expands indefinitely in spite of his efforts to curtail it ; and he may sigh to find that the main outline before him insensibly loses itself in a multitude of necessary details. If he is to tell the truth, he cannot isolate one set of principles or tendencies ; for he knows that many of equal importance were at work at the same time. He is bound to take them all into consideration, and to show their mutual action. What wonder that his book grows in spite of all his efforts to restrain it within definite limits ?

Indeed history, unlike other branches of knowledge, cannot prescribe limitations for itself. It is not only that men need the experience of the past to help them in practical endeavours, to enable them to understand the position of actual questions with which they and their age are engaged. For this purpose accurate facts are needed—not opinions, however plausible, which are unsustained by facts. At the same time, the variety of the matters with which history is bound to concern itself steadily increases. As more interest is taken in questions relating to social organization, researches are conducted in fields which before were neglected. It is useless for the science of history to plead established precedent for its methods, or to refuse to lend itself willingly to the demands made upon its resources. The writer of history has to struggle as he best may with multifarious requirements, which threaten to turn him from a man of letters into the compiler of an encyclopædia.

This continual increase of curiosity, this widening of interest introduces a succession of new subjects for historical research. Documents once disregarded as unimportant are found to yield information as to the silent growth of tendencies which gradually became influential. The mass of letters and papers, increasing at a rate that seems to be accelerated from year to year, offers a continual series of new suggestions. They not only supplement what was known before, but frequently require so much readjustment of previous judgments, that a new presentation of the whole subject becomes necessary. This process goes on without a break, and it is hard in any branch of history to keep pace with the stock of monographs, or illustrations of particular points, which research and industry are constantly producing. However much a writer may strive to know all that can be known, new knowledge is always flowing in. Modern history in this resembles the chief branches of Natural Science; before the results of the last experiments can be tabulated and arranged in their relation to the whole knowledge of the subject, new experiments have been commenced which promise to carry the process still further.

In sciences, however, which deal with nature, the object of research is fixed and stable : it is only man's power of observation that increases. But history deals with a subject which is constantly varying in itself and which is regarded by each succeeding generation from a different point of view. We search the records of the past of mankind, in order that we may learn wisdom for the present, and hope for the future. We wish to discover tendencies which are permanent, ideas which promise to be fruitful, conceptions by which we may judge the course most likely to secure abiding results. We are bound to assume, as the scientific hypothesis on which history is to be written, a progress in human affairs. This progress must inevitably be towards some end ; and we find it difficult to escape the temptation, while we keep that end in view, of treating certain events as great landmarks on the road. A mode of historical presentation thus comes into fashion based upon an inspiring assumption. But the present is always criticizing the past, and events which occur pass judgment on events which have occurred. Time is always revealing the weaknesses of past achievements, and suggesting doubts as to the methods by which they were won. Each generation, as it looks back, sees a change in the perspective, and cannot look with the same eyes as its predecessor.

There are other reasons of a like kind which might further explain the exceeding difficulty of writing a history of modern times on any consecutive plan. The possibility of effective and adequate condensation is almost abandoned, except for rudimentary purposes. The point of view of any individual writer influences not only his judgment of what he presents, but his principle of selection ; and such is the wealth of matter with which the writer of modern history has to deal, that selection is imperative. In the vast and diversified area of modern history, the point of view determines the whole nature of the record, or else the whole work sinks to the level of a mass of details uninformed by any luminous idea. The writer who strives to avoid any tendency becomes dull, and the cult of impartiality paralyses the judgment.

The present work is an attempt to avoid this result on an intelligible system. Every period and every subject has features of its own which strike the mind of the student who has made that period or subject the field of his investigations. His impressions are not derived from previous conceptions of necessary relations between what he has studied and what went before or after ; they are formed directly from the results of his own labours. Round some definite nucleus, carefully selected, these impressions can be gathered together ; and the age can be presented as speaking for itself. No guide is so sure for an historian as an overmastering sense of the importance of events as they appeared to those who took part in them. There can be no other basis on which to found any truly sympathetic treatment.

From this point of view a series of monographs, conceived on a connected system, instead of presenting a collection of fragments, possesses a definite unity of its own. The selection and arrangement of the subjects to be treated provides a general scheme of connection which readily explains itself. Each separate writer treats of a subject with which he is familiar, and is freed from any other responsibility than that of setting forth clearly the salient features of the period or subject entrusted to him. The reader has before him a series of presentations of the most important events and ideas. He may follow any line of investigation of his own, and may supply links of connection at his will. He may receive suggestions from different minds, and may pursue them. He is free from the domination of one intelligence—a domination which has its dangers however great that intelligence may be—striving to express the multifarious experience of mankind in categories of its own creation. He is free at the same time from the aridity of a chronological table—a record of events strung round so slight a thread that no real connection is apparent. Each subject or period has a natural coherence of its own. If this be grasped, its relations to other divisions of the work will be readily apparent and may be followed without difficulty.

This is the main idea on which the method pursued in these volumes is founded. The mode of treatment adopted is not arbitrary, or dictated by considerations of convenience. It springs from the nature of the subject and its difficulties. Specialization is absolutely necessary for the study of history, and it is impossible for any one master mind to co-ordinate in one product the results of all the special work that is being accomplished around it. Elements of interest and suggestiveness, which are of vital importance to the specialist, disappear before the abstract system which the compiler must, whatever may be the scale of his undertaking, frame for his own guidance. The task is too large, its relations are too numerous and too indefinite, for any one mind, however well stored, to appreciate them all. It is better to allow the subject-matter to supply its own unifying principle than to create one which is inadequate or of mere temporary value. At all events, this work has been undertaken with a desire to solve a very difficult problem, and to supply a very real need, so far as was possible under the conditions of its publication.

M. CREIGHTON, Introductory Note, *Cambridge Modern History*, I., pp. 3–6 (1907).

The Scope of History

THE scope of history has gradually widened till it has come to include every aspect of the life of humanity. No one would now dare to maintain with Seeley that history was the biography of States, and with Freeman that it was merely past politics. The growth of nations, the achievements of men of action, the rise and fall of parties remain among the most engrossing themes of the historian; but he now casts his net wider and embraces the whole record of civilization. The influence of nature, the pressure of economic factors, the origin and transformation of ideas, the contribution of science and art, religion and philosophy, literature and law, the material conditions of life, the fortunes of the masses—such problems now claim his attention in no less degree. He must see life steadily and see it whole.

G. P. GOOCH, *History and Historians in the
Nineteenth Century,* p. 573.

The Case for Modern History

THE modernists, if I may call them so, have been reproached for pandering to modern fashions and anxieties. They have been accused of erring into fields of history where no definitive work can be done for want of full and authentic information, and where it is inevitable that they should abandon the proper work of the historian for the more dubious office of the partisan or the prophet. I myself am one of the offenders, since for ten years at least I have devoted an increasing proportion of my time to modern history. Some of my friends think that I am making a mistake. They may be right, but so far they have not convinced me. On behalf of myself, and of others who stand in the same position, I ask your indulgence while I state the case for modern history. But before I do so, let me disclaim any thought of depreciating mediæval studies. Next to Ancient History they supply the finest discipline that can be offered to the historical beginner. The patient study of mediæval texts trains the critical faculty and trains the historical imagination. The religious and ethical and political ideas of the Middle Ages are of the greatest interest and importance, not only by reason of the influence which they still exercise upon the modern world, but also as constituting a system which satisfied the mind and the conscience and the religious instincts of Europe for at least four hundred years. And for one purpose or another the laws and the institutions of the Middle Ages will long remain fruitful subjects of research. The problems which they suggest will always appeal to many serious investigators. But there are many minds to which modern history makes a more urgent appeal. Is it not legitimate, is it not proper and necessary, that modern history, even the history of the nineteenth century, should be studied as patiently and scientifically as that of the Middle Ages ? . . . In practice there is a disposition to take the view, diametrically opposed to the view of Bolingbroke and Chesterfield and

Chatham, that historical studies must become less scientific, less educational, the more nearly they approach to modern times. The eighteenth-century statesman took a prejudiced, a narrow view of history. But is there not also a prejudice and narrowness in this other view which was so much affected by the nineteenth-century historian ? I will not detain you with lengthy proofs that the most jealously guarded materials for nineteenth-century history are fast becoming available. I will only remark that less than a year ago the archives of the Foreign Office were made accessible to students up till the year 1878 ; that the military and state archives of Vienna are accessible up till 1895 ; and that a vast mass of the official correspondence of Bismarck as Imperial Chancellor and his successors has recently been published by the German Foreign Office. Other, less confidential, but not less valuable documents for foreign and for British history are pouring on us every year. Are we to leave it entirely to the casual reviewer to take stock of the new information ? The discreet modernist will not vex himself overmuch with the problems presented by the history of yesterday or the day before. Neither will he be so sanguine as to suppose that a definitive account of any part of the nineteenth century can yet be written. But many provisional accounts must be written, an immense amount of material must be sifted critically, before some historian yet unborn can give us a complete and rounded narrative. It is not given to all of us to write prose epics. For the humbler minded, whose ambition is simply to enlarge the empire of sound knowledge, there is spade work enough and more than enough to be done in the nineteenth century.

We modernists are influenced by the trend of opinion among educated men and women. They wish to know more about the history of this nation and of other European nations since the Napoleonic wars. Is it beneath the dignity of the historian to satisfy this demand? Should he not have the present in his mind when he is working on the past? Should he not take some account of the needs of his own generation? Let it be granted— the most inveterate of moderns will grant—that modern conditions must often be explained by reference to a remote past that lies far behind the battle of Waterloo ; that some of our modern doubts and questionings may be more completely answered by reference to Thucydides and other political thinkers of the ancient world, than by the study of blue-books and debates and memoirs. Let it be granted that the nineteenth century is no more self-contained and self-begotten than any other era ; and that those who know nothing before 1815 will not be in a position to say much that is instructive about anything that follows after. Are these sufficient reasons for discountenancing special studies which commence about that year? I should be sorry to think so. For of this I am sure. Whether we like these modern periods or not, they are being studied and will continue to be studied outside our Universities by those who are not in a position to form sound historical opinions for themeslves, who are very much at the mercy of uninstructed and unbalanced teachers. If modern history is

not studied and written by those whose one aim
is to discover and to relate the truth, it will fall
into the hands of writers whose objects are less
worthy.

> H. W. C. DAVIS, " The Study of History," an
> Inaugural Lecture, 1925. (See *Henry William
> Carless Davis, 1874–1928*, pp. 70–72, ed.
> J. R. H. Weaver and A. L. Poole.)

Goose Clubs, Spikenard, and Mastic

IF the economic historian has his modesties in
presence of the pure economist he also has his
pride. He is proud because, by definition as
historian, he is one to whom the tangled variety
of human life is attractive in itself ; one who will
study alterations in the tangle for the love of it,
even when his information is such that he can
never hope to pick out with assurance the forces at
work, or measure exactly the changes brought
about by the aggregate of them between dates x and
y. He cares for the beginnings of things as such.
He likes to trace the growth of institutions which
have been moulded by man's need to keep alive
and man's desire for comfort and prosperity—
village communities, trading companies, Christ-
mas goose clubs—although he may not be able to
number the community, read the balance sheet of
the company, or find the slate of the goose club. It
pleases him to know that in such and such an age
caravans took the golden road to Samarkand, and
that in such another age they went no more, even
if he cannot count the camels or prove—what he
always suspects—that the total amount of the

rose-candy, spikenard, and mastic conveyed was really trifling. Some men—George Unwin was one—have turned to economic history mainly because it is so full of workings together for useful ends, of community life of all sorts, not because it is particularly rich—as, of course, it is —in " entities with a metrical aspect." Others may like best what is odd, individual, idiosyncratic in the story of how men have kept alive and as comfortable as may be. It is, in fact, a story full of attractive oddities. They weary of the general averages of statistical truth and of such human sequences as may be plotted in graphs. Others again may care most for the unmeasurable thoughts which make the measured things. But these all are within the covenant, very well within it. The historian likes his companions to be as varied as his matter ; and happily there is no excluding definition which says that to be economic an " entity " must be " metrical."

J. H. CLAPHAM, The Study of Economic History,
pp. 34–36.

The Case for Medieval History

I WAS brought up in a tradition of medieval studies, and I have no intention of deserting it. I make no extravagant or exclusive claims on behalf of this tradition, although I think that earnest attention to medieval history is the best preparation for the specialist in any field of later history, not because it offers a picturesque invitation to the dormant historical faculty, but by reason of its austere disciplinary value and its penetrating ever-present influence upon our modern life. I am not sure that since the war the nearness of the Middle Ages has not been more apparent. The outlook of Dante is in some ways more natural to us than the outlook of Hobbes, although while much in the *De Monarchia* continues to repel or even disgust us, the delicious absurdities and the engaging pedantry in seventeenth-century thought will always amuse us. But, quite apart from the mental and spiritual results of recent events, there is no doubt that during the last generation the medieval world has become much more real and intelligible to us. For one thing, the setting of medieval history is different to-day. It is one thing to reveal the vast stretches of time during which human life was struggling to order itself before Rome was founded, to reduce the thousand years of the medieval societies to a mere episode in the history of mankind ; it is another to fill in the background. It is one thing to insist upon the continuity of history and the organic treatment of the development of national institutions ; it is another to trace the influences which played upon the medieval world, and the persistent sur-vivals of medieval habits of life and outlook into later centuries. Thirty years ago we were familiar enough with the former processes of scholarship, and I should be the last to underestimate their significance. Sir Francis Palgrave's wise Preface to his *History of Normandy and England*, written in 1851, and much in Guizot's fine work, and Freeman's teaching, and the spirit as well as most of the letter of Stubbs, are as true to-day as they were then. But the scholarship of the last forty or fifty years has gradually given life and meaning to principles, and bridged the gap between the historical imagination and historical truth. We are prepared to find a greater variety in medieval life, to see medieval society as we see our own, more as self-conscious, constructive, receptive, complex, less as the half-awake creature of habit. We can regard the Middle Ages more in the manner of Tocqueville, not so much in the manner of Maine. The change in the setting has led to a revision of the contents.

Take, for example, the development of Byzantine studies. For about eight hundred years the Eastern Empire was not merely the chief Christian state in the world ; it was the only state comparable to Persia, and later to the Caliphate, able to profit on equal terms by intercourse with them. While by its existence it protected the western communities, it was a clearing-house in which they could become acquainted with the treasures of the East. So far from being a moribund society of decadent voluptuaries and half-imbecile theologians, it was the greatest, most active and most enduring political organism that the world has yet seen, giving for centuries that opportunity for living which we associate with the spacious but transitory peace of Augustus or Hadrian. The recognition of all this has been the result of the scholarship of the last half-century, so that with some exaggeration we tend now to give to the Empire the sort of significance in the development of the West as we give to Venice in the story of medieval trade or to Glasgow in the life of the Scottish Highlands. The indirect results of re-statements of this kind are even more important. We realize that medieval peoples could be taken out of themselves. Their absorption in their own beliefs and customs, their efforts to reconcile the teaching of Christian missionaries with their own traditions, were disturbed by visions of material and artistic splendour and influenced by fresh movements of the mind. They became more sophisticated and in course of time creative. And in adopting this point of view we are led on to find new values in activities of the schools, of men of letters, of the workshops, which were at one time regarded as somewhat remote from the normal course of medieval political life.

All the same, we shall never cease to argue about the meaning and the value of things in the Middle Ages. Amidst so much that seems familiar to us, there is something which escapes us, and which we feel must always escape us. This aloofness is felt most in that central period—the Middle Ages proper—which passes into a more friendly age in the middle of the fourteenth century. Just when they are most expressive, they are most withdrawn, and as it were most indifferent to us. It was a wonderful, but to us it appears as an uncomfortable, time. I should be more at ease listening to Dr. Johnson for an hour than sitting in the classroom of Aquinas. I once heard a well-known novelist say, at the end of a paper on Dante, that if the poet were to enter the room, he would go out of it. This perhaps was ex-cessive, but I at any rate should withdraw into a corner. What is it that draws us to such an age, quite apart from the lessons which can be derived from it ? Why should a man be more thrilled by the Paris of Abelard than by the Paris of Molière, more moved by the career of Simon de Montfort than by the exploits of Nelson ? Shepherds have kept their sheep in all ages : why am I stirred so deeply because I can trace the very sheep-walks of the monks of Furness ? Why is there a remote, yet strangely familiar, music about the names of places—Beverley, Gainsborough, Thrapston, Tewkesbury—a music in which it is impossible to distinguish the call of authentic English speech from the echoes of a hundred insistent associations ? This is more than an obstinate survival of the splendid, if ignorant, excitement of the romantic movement. It is unprovoked, with no heat or enthusiasm driving us beside ourselves. It grows with knowledge, as the familiar becomes more accessible, and the remote more sharply defined in its aloofness from us. It is the sense of the past which comes to us from the Middle Ages as it came to the young American in Henry James's story, as he wandered about his eighteenth-century house in London—the sense of a " conscious past, recognizing no less than recognizable." The place was a museum, " but a museum of held reverberations." So long as we are conscious of these " held reverberations," history will continue to entice us. So long as their mystery endures, and it will always endure, the past will continue to escape us.

F. M. POWICKE, *Historical Study in Oxford,*
pp. 21–24.

Chronicles and Official Records

TIME was when the chronicle was considered the sole or the main material for mediæval history. A now-forgotten history of the Norman Conquest declared itself on the title-page to be based on a " new collation of the contemporary chronicles." Few writers would be so naïve nowadays as to regard as adequate such a facile method of historical composition. With the opening up of archives and with their contents becoming more accessible through lists, calendars, summaries and the publication *in extenso* of many documents, it has become the fashion to regard the record as superior in authority to the chronicle. There is now a school of historians which is not satisfied unless it can base its conclusions on record evidence. Some of its extreme disciples act as if records could never be wrong. They often declare that chroniclers are essentially untrustworthy. It is easy to demonstrate the unwisdom of such extreme claims. It is more important to notice that, with the increased study of records, the chronicle has more or less come under a cloud.

The consequences of this reaction have been the more serious since with the increased study of records has come a widened view of the province of history. It is not so very long ago that Freeman said, amidst general approval, that history was past politics and politics present history. But nowadays our conception of history is not limited to the history of the state. Even when we still fix our attention on political history, our object is not primarily to frame a narrative. We wish to describe, to analyse, to reconstruct, to understand, rather than simply to tell the tale in chronological sequence. And some of the more ardent souls are beginning to despise political history altogether. They seek to expound not the the history of the state but the history of society; and rightly, since in modern and even in mediæval times the state was not the only, or even the most potent of the organizations which bound together man and man for a common purpose. With this extension of the field of history, the chronicler becomes less important. He is, above all things, the teller of a story. If history is not primarily narrative, what is the use of the chronicler?

The exclusive cult of the chronicler was one-sided and unscientific; but the excessive reaction against him cannot be justified, either by the importance of other sources of information, or by the inclusion within the historic field of activities with which the political or the narrative historian has little concern. Nor can we study the history of society with effect until we have set forth clearly the history of the state in all its aspects. And of how many periods of our mediæval history can we truly say that the basis of political history has been well and truly laid? And where would political history be if it were not for the chronicles?

T. F. Tout, " The Study of Mediæval Chronicles,"
Collected Papers, III., p. 17 (1920).

The Case for World History

THE *Outline of History*, of which this is a fourth edition, freshly revised and rearranged, is an attempt to tell, truly and clearly, in one continuous narrative, the whole story of life and mankind so far as it is known to-day. It is written plainly for the general reader, but its aim goes beyond its use as merely interesting reading matter. There is a feeling abroad that the teaching of history considered as a part of general education is in an unsatisfactory condition, and particularly that the ordinary treatment of this " subject " by the class and teacher and examiner is too partial and narrow. But the desire to extend the general range of historical ideas is confronted by the argument that the available time for instruction is already consumed by that partial and narrow treatment, and that therefore, however desirable the extension of range may be, it is in practice impossible. If an Englishman, for example, has found the history of England quite enough for his powers of assimilation, then it seems hopeless to expect his sons and daughters to master universal history, if that is to consist of the history of England, plus the history of France, plus the history of Germany, plus the history of Russia, and so on. To which the only possible answer is that universal history is at once something more and something less than the aggregate of the national histories to which we are accustomed, that it must be approached in a different spirit and dealt with in a different manner. This book seeks to fortify that answer. It has been written primarily to show that *history as one whole* is amenable to a more broad and comprehensive handling than is the history of special nations and periods, a broader handling that will bring it within the normal limitations of time and energy set to the reading and education of an ordinary citizen. This outline deals with ages and races and nations where the ordinary history deals with reigns and pedigrees and campaigns ; but it will not be found to be more crowded with names and dates, nor more difficult to follow and understand. History is no exception amongst the sciences ; as the gaps fill in, the outline simplifies ; as the outlook broadens, the clustering multitude of details dissolves into general laws. And many topics of quite primary interest to mankind, the first appearance and the growth of scientific knowledge for example, and its effects upon human life, the elaboration of the ideas of money and credit, or the story of the origins and spread and influence of Christianity, which must be treated fragmentarily or by elaborate digressions in any partial history, arise and flow completely and naturally in one general record of the world in which we live.

The need for a common knowledge of the general facts of human history throughout the world has become very evident during the tragic happenings of the last few years. Swifter means of communication have brought all men closer to one another for good or for evil. War becomes a universal disaster, blind and monstrously destructive ; it bombs the baby in its cradle and sinks the food-ships that cater for the non-combatant and the neutral. There can be no peace now, we realize, but a common peace in all the world ; no prosperity but a general prosperity. But there can be no common peace and prosperity without common historical ideas. Without such ideas to hold them together in harmonious co-operation, with nothing but narrow, selfish, and conflicting nationalist traditions, races and peoples are bound to drift towards conflict and destruction. This truth, which was apparent to that great philosopher Kant a century or more ago—it is the gist of his tract upon universal peace—is now plain to the man in the street. Our internal politics and our economic and social ideas are profoundly vitiated at present by wrong and fantastic ideas of the origin and historical relationship of social classes. A sense of history as the common adventure of all mankind is as necessary for peace within as it is for peace between the nations.

H. G. WELLS, *The Outline of History*, Introd.

The Economic Interpretation of History

HISTORY is an account of the things that mattered most in the past, and it derives its chief interest from the assumption that those things were largely the causes of what matters to us now. And, if the things that matter most are the same now as then, the assumption seems natural. To Seeley, the British Empire is what matters most now—the central result of history. Looking back over the eighteenth century, he finds that " the great events are all foreign wars." These at first seem a chaotic imbroglio. But if we steadily ignore much that seems to lead nowhere and much that leads in the opposite direction, we soon perceive a chain of historic causation leading to one great result, and thus History becomes a science and Imperialism a religion.

But, if what matters most to us now is not Empire, but class conflicts and the interests of Labour, we are driven to re-explore history, and to dig for these aspects of the past beneath the political surface, where we shall certainly find them. The stimulus of discovery and the discipline of a higher criticism combine to give "Industrial History" a high educational value, and they account for some of its popularity, but not for all. The deeper reason is to be found in the belief that, behind what seemed to matter most to the historians, we are getting at what really mattered most to most people in the past, and that these things are casually connected with what matters most to most people of to-day. The economic interpretation of history thus claims to be at once scientific and religious.

I am glad to find that other tutors agree with me in rejecting this economic interpretation as inadequate, but the search for some scientific, religious, or philosophic interpretation is what gives the strongest interest to our subject, and, even if we cannot fully direct it, we need not disown it. I find it best to meet this explicit attitude of faith with a *confessio fidei* of my own. I believe in the spiritual interpretation of history. I hold, that is to say, that the central and ultimate subject of history lies in the development of the inward possessions and experiences of men, through religion, art, literature, science, music, philosophy, but above all, through the deepening and widening of ordinary social communications.

Social history in this full sense, though concerned with prime realities, is itself an ideal. Political history, as actually written, is concerned largely with illusions. Our task as scholars and teachers lies between the two. We have to build up the New Jerusalem with one hand and repair the old Jericho with the other. But where does economic history come in ? I answer that it provides a foothold in actualities, and an approach on the right hand and on the left to the Jerusalem and Jericho of social and political history.

Social history should be concerned with Life, Truth, and Beauty—with the energizing souls of men in community ; and these are ends in themselves. Political history and economic history are concerned with means to social ends, and with the enormous abuse of those means perverted to such ends as power and wealth. They are largely a story of destruction and waste, disguised as constructive achievements till they end in unmistakable catastrophe, and counteracted by vitalizing social forces of which history as yet takes little or no account. The deeper causes of this ever-recurrent collapse of civilization are moral and social, but the immediate symptoms and clues to the pathological process are economic. " Great is bankruptcy," cries Carlyle, as he contemplates the end of the *ancien régime*. Professor Firth, in his account of Cromwell's finance, lays a more scientific finger on the same place. But a *post-mortem* autopsy is not enough ; we need diagnosis of the patient at an earlier stage, and this the professed economic historian should supply. The story of taxation, direct and indirect, of the anticipation of revenue, of war debts, and of the rise of a *rentier* class provides the main clue to the reactions of State policy upon Western societies from the early days of the Italian republics till now.

. . . .

So much for the critical approach which economic history furnishes to political history. The approach to social history is of a more directly constructive kind. Class conflict, which is a very real factor in history—Marx is more scientific than Seeley—and the class interests which account for most social legislation, are not constructive forces ; but they are evidences of a creative evolution in communities, which is, I think, the central positive aspect of history. The economic historian finds what is, perhaps, his main task in the study of communities of life and kinship, of work and vocation, of property and enterprise, *on the side of their economic results*. Adequately to account for, or at any rate to formulate, the emergence of new forms of community, new social species, implied in the growing complexity and fluidity of class relations, is the chief task of social history, as of social science and of social philosophy.

To those who distrust the *a priori* approach to these subjects, the discipline which we call economic history provides an *a posteriori* approach along the solid causeway of objective fact.

G. UNWIN, " Economic History in Tutorial Classes,"
Collected Papers, ed. R. H. Tawney, pp. 37–39.

Historical Realities

THE book itself has grown out of an original plan of three or four introductory chapters for the second volume of *Five Centuries of Religion*. It is impossible fully to understand St. Francis without measuring the extent to which his gospel was a revolt against the capitalism of the older Orders. And, apart from this, we can never estimate the religion of any age or society without observing its attitude towards the poor. But this observation must be two-fold ; rich and poor react upon each other ; to understand the monk as land-lord, we must realize something of peasant life in general : and thus my preliminary sketch has grown to a size which demands separate publica-tion. Yet it remains, in substance, an intro-ductory essay, designed to break ground in this field and to redress an unequal balance in mediæval historiography. Sooner or later, we must out-grow what may almost be called the present monopoly of constitutional theory and social theory ; sooner or later, we must struggle to discover not only what men were organized to do six centuries ago, and not only what the academic publicists of that age prescribed for them to do, but what they actually did and suffered ; and, by the way, what they themselves actually thought of the civil and ecclesiastical constitutions, or the social theories, under which they had to live. Not, of course, that there is any hard-and-fast line between constitutional and social history ; they overlap and illustrate each other at every turn. Yet there is a real difference ; each needs special study in the light of its own special records ; neither has dictatorial rights over the other ; and for an author to draw easy inferences from one to the other, without continual reference to actual documents, must always be hazardous and is often grossly misleading. . . . The one value of history is, that it should deal with realities ; and a system which deliberately confines research to one particular fraction of the ascertainable realities—which puts concrete facts, so to speak, upon its *Index Expurgatorius*—can only lead to disaster in the long run. I am giving my readers, therefore, as many concrete facts as time and space will permit. Let others take account of the evidence here produced, adding to it and correcting it where necessary, and suggesting any working theory not irreconcilable with these facts. For no theory is put forward in these pages but as a challenge to serious future inquiry ; many of the points, it is plain, need much further special study ; I only plead that they should be studied not *in vacuo*, but in the light of actual documentary evidence, which may be found by all who care to seek.

G. G. COULTON, *The Mediæval Village,* ix., x.

The Case for Local History

UNTIL a comparatively short time ago . . . the study of local history was left almost entirely to the antiquary. The professional historian, occupied with politics and the fortunes of great nations, had no time for surveying the more humble corners of his field in detail. These were left, for the most part, to a band of workers full of enthusiasm and local patriotism, but often without training or special fitness, who did much valuable and enlightened work, but, on the other hand, through their inexperience, frequently bequeathed a disastrous heritage to their followers. To-day there is a change. There are signs everywhere that the antiquary is realizing the claim which history has upon him, and that he is losing the point of view from which he was accustomed to isolate the objects of his interest and magnify their unique importance. While he, on the one hand, is awaking to the fact that the ultimate worth of the pains which he expends upon the annals of a single village, or even upon the growth of a single building, is their contribution to the illustration of national and social progress, the historian, on the other, is turning more and more to local records and monuments, as furnishing an indispensable and hitherto somewhat neglected part of his regular equipment. The antiquary is graduating in history, and the historian is competing with antiquaries upon their own ground ; each is redeeming his previous inferiority with great advantage to both parties.

Indeed, among those historians who occupy themselves specially with constitutional and social history, there is a growing feeling that the general history of their subject has been written on the large scale, and that the task of future writers lies in the minute revision of detail. If the scholar aspires to be a discoverer, he must penetrate into those odd angles which have been overlooked or imperfectly explored. This is so true of certain periods in history that there is a tendency on the part of the conservative historian, who is intent upon the wider aspect of his theme, to condemn absorption in all but recent history as mere antiquarianism, narrowing and obscuring historical vision. The danger foreseen by such critics is obvious, especially where it involves the early training of students on minutely specialized lines. At the same time, we cannot but welcome the fact that the pursuits of antiquaries are becoming of increasing importance to historical scholars, not only as objects of casual and intelligent attention, but as part of their own recognized programme.

Local history, from the lofty point of view, may be mere antiquarianism. It deals largely with the ancient and obsolete, with institutions that have seen their best days, families that have passed into oblivion, buildings which in the course of years have lost all likeness to their original selves. Further, it is inevitable that local history should remain to some extent in the hands of the local antiquary. He possesses, or at any rate is the only person likely to possess, the necessary topographical knowledge, for want of which the most accomplished alien has often been known to come to grief. But there are other essentials which he should command ; training in the discriminating use of documents, a comparative knowledge which extends well beyond the limits of his own district, and the sense of proportion which enables him to use his miscellaneous material to the best advantage. It is seldom, even now, that all these can be found together, and, even when they are, we do not always value the local antiquary as much as we ought. His pursuits are not lucrative ; the more immersed in them he becomes, the more expensive he finds them. The person who should regard them as a road to fame and fortune must be very astute or very sanguine ; and such persons are not found outside fiction, where it is usually by nefarious or doubtful means that they obtain an insecure eminence in their profession. The methods even of that great man, Baptist Hatton, in Disraeli's *Sybil*, the master of pedigrees and the effortless reviver of extinct and dormant peerages, were not above suspicion. Such super-antiquaries exist only in the imagination, and the immodest competencies in which they flourish are beyond the capacity of the mere seeker after truth. If the local antiquary can be said to flourish it is upon interests which are their own reward, and I am afraid that he is often looked upon with a wonder that has nothing in it akin to respect by that section of the world which regards itself as possessing the monopoly of practical wisdom.

.   .   .   .

In conclusion, I may ask leave to enumerate the points which seem to me most worthy of consideration with regard to this topic of village history.

First, it is history in a very special sense. The history of every village, we are often told, is a microcosm of the history of England. Not that it has much to do with political events. The inhabitants of Gridlington Magna, so far as I can conjecture (for I have no facts to go upon), displayed no emotion when they heard that the Great Charter had been signed. They were probably very sluggish in waking up to the progress of the Reformation. Towton and Marston Moor affected them as little as they affected Totnes or Marazion. All the time, however, there were working in the village and parish those economic forces that are at the root of history, and there was growing up in various forms and in a succession of phases the machinery of local government, with all the ties that bind it to the central authority. If this point is kept in sight, the history of Gridlington may be made in very truth for its inhabitants the history of England— a social and economic record of the utmost value.

Secondly, apart from this, there are certain essential features in the history of a village which need to be recorded, intimately connected as they are with its prosperity and social order. Here, again, the difficulty of making the political facts of English history hinge upon Gridlington is clearly apparent. If Sir Pain stood with King Richard in sight of the Holy City, if Sir Anketel fell beside Simon de Montfort at Evesham, if Sir John, whom Leland confounded with Old King Cole, sought to moderate the Black Prince's rage at Limoges, these are useful pegs upon which to hang more general matters. But what are we to say of that long period of inactivity and apparent indifference to national affairs which lasted until Sir Toby journeyed to Exeter to show his loyalty to William of Orange ? We may, indeed, indulge in sentimental fiction after this fashion : " Doubtless Sir Ralph as he rode out of the courtyard of the old manor-house, then, as now, weather-worn and stained with lichen, on his way to the assizes at Bunchester, felt a genuine sentiment of pride in his inheritance, and thankfully murmured to himself the family motto, *Funes mihi ceciderunt in præclaris*. Ye lotte is fallen unto me in a fayre ground." Or we may go into detail in a more plausible style as follows : " We are informed by our learned friend, the Rev. Mr. Dusty, that after a prolonged and exhaustive search among the records of the diocese, he has been unable to discover any intimation of the institution of Nicholas Flytermous to the rectory of Gridlington. In spite of this unfortunate omission we know that the troubles of the reign of Richard II. left him untouched. Undisturbed by the catastrophe of Redcot Bridge, unmoved, as far as we know, by the tragic fate of the Duke of Gloucester, out of the path of Bolingbroke as he pursued his unresisted march from the Humber to the Cotswolds, Nicholas appears to have lived to a hale old age and to have died in 1420, two years before the victor of Agincourt gave up the ghost in the castle of Vincennes. In lack of positive evidence to the contrary, may we not conclude that Nicholas Flytermous was a worthy imitator of those Christian virtues practised so notably by Chaucer's parson ? Would it be wrong to indulge the fancy that Chaucer himself one early morning, wandering far afield in his devotion to the awakening daisy, encountered upon the uplands of Gridlington Down this excellent priest hastening to church at the sound of the day-bell, and enshrined the reminiscence imperishably in his portrait of the Parson ? "

We may answer that it would be quite wrong. But such nonsense has often been, and is still occasionally written, and I am afraid that people are sometimes taken in by it. It is much easier to weave fancies than to tell the sober truth. And the truth in village history is very sober. There is the main line of historical fact. We must have questions of ownership firmly defined ; we must have the descent of the manorial rights and privileges with the history of the advowson of the parish church. For these things we shall have to go to official documents, for the most part in the Public Record Office ; and these documents will often provide details which may be used to fill in and complete the picture of manorial organization which it will be our endeavour to elicit from the bare facts. The history of the great house and of the church of the village are closely interwoven with its economic history ; they help to illustrate the transition from feudalism to modern conditions, the progress of freedom slowly broadening down from precedent to precedent. If the historian works conscientiously with this before his eyes, his devotion to a corner of the field of history will satisfy the most archæologically minded professor of the art, while his enlightened view of the scope of his theme will go far to meet the severe requirements of the modernist.

"Local History," by Professor A. Hamilton Thompson,
in *Transactions of the Bristol and Gloucestershire
Archæological Society, 1926*, XLVIII., pp. 57–74.

Changing Views

No one who has followed the results of historical inquiry during the last generation can have failed to be impressed by their dissolving influence upon some of the older assumptions, which were regarded as axiomatic truths. One of these assumptions was that society as a whole has passed through a series of well-defined stages : the pastoral stage ; the stage of the tribe settled on the land, yet still bound together by tribal ties ; the stage of tribal monarchies ; the feudal stage ; the stage of Parliamentary institutions or estates. Now this assumption is, of course, roughly correct. For example, it is true on the whole to say that the period in which the sense of national unity found expression through a bureaucratic civil service and representative institutions, followed and grew out of the stage in which the source of unity was the feudal court. What is misleading in this belief in definite stages is the further implication that it was impossible for any large or influential element in society to rise above, or to stand apart from, the outlook and habits which are regarded as proper to the

stage in which it is living. Or again, it is generally assumed that ideas and practices which are
associated in our minds with a later, could not
have existed in an earlier stage of society. Beneath
all these assumptions can be seen at work the
influence of the old belief, that man as a social
being has developed rapidly and regularly from a
primitive to a sophisticated and artificial life,
within a comparatively brief time. It is probable
that this view, in its turn, is simply another form
of the mediæval conception of history, as a series
of ages designed by Providence. The realization
that the history of civilized man, and of the
interplay of primitive and sophisticated influences,
has to be carried back for thousands of years, is
profoundly affecting this older view of history.
The story of any modern people, or at any rate
of any modern society in Europe, is now seen to
be a brief episode in a very long and irregular
process. At every point, from the beginning to
the present day, it is found to have been exposed
to all kinds of external influences, and to have
responded within itself in all kinds of unexpected
ways. Hence when we find men of all kinds,
and ideas of all degrees of crudity and subtlety,
at work in all the accepted stages of a people's
history, we are no longer perplexed, we no longer
feel compelled to explain the facts away, or to
deny them altogether. We are not puzzled, for
example, when we find instances of private buying
and selling of land, during a stage which is
supposed to be characterized by tribal custom.
Or again, we are not, or need not be, shaken by
the prevalence of all kinds of credit, in an age

which ought, on the accepted view, to have been familiar with nothing more advanced than payments in kind or in ready money. The same is true of political ideas, and of persons. We have spoken far too glibly of the spirit of an age, or of men of their time. It is now being realized that at all times in the history of Europe there have been men with profound minds, just as there have been men who could not grasp more than the commonplaces of their circle. At all times there have been religious men, in the deepest sense of the word religious, and there have been men who were merely conventionally religious. At all times there have been good men, able to shape their course in accordance with conscious principle, and ordinary men, influenced merely by habit and circumstance.

.   .   .   .

It is possible to go even further, and to trace among primitive and disorderly peoples, no less than among more advanced nations, the controlling guidance of a few great ideas. It is very easy, even in what seem to be the most spontaneous and popular expressions of story and design, in folk-lore, and in vulgar superstition, to overlook the element of the literary and the sophisticated. It has been said that all the fairy stories in the world can ultimately be traced back to the few Indian types. Certainly it is impossible at any point to eradicate the indirect effect upon the mediæval mind of ideas and motives drawn from the Scriptures, the great fathers of the Church, the scientific conceptions and fancies of the Greeks, and the traditions of Roman law and procedure. And behind all these themselves, the finer expression of them, were the more abstract ideas which ultimately guided the destinies of men. These ideas were coherent ; there was, it has been well said, nothing vague. " It was not a question of admirable maxims, but of definite procedure to put things right, and to keep them there. . . . The very anarchy quickened the sense of coherent system." And this mental system was inspired by " the inexpugnable belief that every detailed occurrence can be correlated with its antecedents in a perfectly definite manner exemplifying general principles." It does not matter that only a few minds could attain this vision ; the point is that in this vision what we call the Middle Ages found a controlling purpose. There was something big, to which every man or woman with a capacity for bigness could respond.

F. M. POWICKE, *Mediæval England*, pp. 7–14.

The Variety of Economic History

THE work which economic historians are doing presents a spectacle of rich variety. We may distinguish a number of directions in which the detailed work is tending to become more and more subdivided by specialization, and although none of them is independent of the rest, each has its own problems and its own close relations with workers whom we cannot classify as both economists and historians, some of whom indeed are neither. There is, for instance, the history of technology, of tools and machines, of the chemical and other processes of production and transport. This is indisputably related to our subject; indeed it is more than that, it is a part of our subject. It is a fundamental principle of the evolution of industry that a change of tools or machines brings with it a change of business organization and of the human relationships which that dictates. Yet in finding out what the development of industrial technique has been, we must go far from the beaten path of historical studies. We must see the material evidence preserved for us in museums, and we must do archæological field-work in the often deserted and almost forgotten mills or forges of earlier centuries. We must visit modern mines, factories, workshops, farms. We must gather information and ideas from engineers, from chemists, from geologists. For a long time the history of technology has had a life of its own. From the beginning of the nineteenth century there were German writers who attempted comprehensive and systematic surveys of it as a whole, and the existence of great technological institutes tends to keep it together. In England we have a publishing society, still young but promising, the Newcomen Society, which covers the whole field; but the complexity of modern processes of manufacture and transport is so great that this department in itself is now rather a group of special studies than a subject which single workers can master.

It has become the fashion lately to talk about "business history" as another specialized sectional study. The expression is ambiguous, and it seems to mean sometimes the history of separate firms or businesses, sometimes the history of business in a somewhat wider sense, of business methods and organization. Clearly the unit, to be studied to the best advantage, must be taken in its environment as one business among many, and there are more ways than one in which the story of a single business may be made to illustrate a general development. There are business histories in the heroic or epic manner, of which the theme is the rise of the good man to riches. Others, such as the history of one of our great amalgamated banks, are largely genealogical, and provide useful information on the composition of the business classes in the last three hundred years. The *differentia* of " business history " is, in fact, to be sought not in its method or point of view so much as in its materials : it is history based on the records of business itself, as distinguished from the information about business collected by governments or tabulated by economists and statisticians. In a sense material of this sort has long been in use. Account-books, for instance, provided Thorold Rogers with the bulk of his facts ; but in recent years their use has changed. Rogers used them mainly as sources of information about thousands of separate transactions. He split them up and tabulated them. Attention is turned now rather to the total effects of the transactions on those who made them, to the fortunes and methods of persons and firms, the structure of economic life. A great store of materials of this kind, from the business archives of the Medici and still earlier traders down to our own time, is waiting to be explored and used.

It is important that what is worth keeping shall be preserved, and that the process of destruction, which has been very active among these superficially unattractive papers, shall be checked. In several countries, whether by the formation of societies or otherwise, there is a commendable movement for building up repositories in which business firms may place their records for the use of students. We in England are sometimes accused of being backward in this, but we have made a beginning and the time has come for pressing on with the work. In several universities and public libraries there are growing collections of this sort, and we may reasonably mention along with them the repositories of Lord Hanworth's national scheme for storing manorial records, of which one is the Bodleian. These manorial documents are nominally legal but in fact mainly economic, and, thanks to them, English agrarian history can be studied in minute detail for a long period of time. We have every reason to be proud also of the records of the East India Company, and especially of the great series of published volumes from them for the seventeenth century. The Bank of England is more secretive, even about its earliest days. Let us hope that it will allow us to thaw out the frozen records in its vaults. I cannot conceive of a good reason why any existing firm, whether semi-public or purely private, should be reluctant to throw open the whole of its records down at least to the year 1870.

.   .   .   .

And here, as a corrective to the impression of bewildering variety in economic history, I would put on record a half-humorous remark which was thrown out in conversation by the late Professor H. W. C. Davis. " Economic history," he said, " is that kind of history which requires a knowledge of economics." This may seem an austere definition. It excludes much entertaining gossip about " the olden times " which has passed for economic history. But it provides a criterion for deciding what we ought to investigate and what we may leave aside, and to that extent it lightens and simplifies our task. It is not indeed possible, and it would not be desirable, for the theorist to tell the historian exactly what to look for, or for the historian to furnish the theorist with exactly the information which he wants. That would be possible only if a satisfactory theory could be constructed with a number of blanks into which there would afterwards obediently fit themselves illustrative or corroborative facts. As it is, the facts will dictate or contain their own interpretation, and theory will unite with history in an equal partnership. Neither will be merely ancillary and neither a mere external check on the other. In the last resort the two studies cannot, as I believe, logically be distinguished. Historians for their part ought to try to maintain a close co-operation between them. Only theory can deliver us from mere antiquarianism or aimless curiosity and make research what it ought to be, a methodical advance from the known, through the unknown, to what is worth knowing.

G. N. CLARK, " The Study of Economic History," in *History*, XVII., No. 66 (July 1932), pp. 97–110.

The History of Civilization

" CIVILIZATION " is one of the most comprehensive of the words under which we group together human activities, and it is often used so loosely that when we talk about the civilization of a period we mean everything that men did in that period. This book is intended to give a summary account of Western civilization in the seventeenth century, but not in any such loose and indefinite sense. It does not attempt to survey every department of human life. On the contrary, it has a definite subject and a definite point of view. It takes, one by one, a number of the more important activities, and tries to show in what ways they were, at that period of time, mutually connected. In this task two opposite errors have to be avoided. There is the danger which besets the limited or superficial historian, of thinking that any one of these subjects can be adequately treated as a self-contained whole by itself. Economic history, military history, the history of science, each of these branches is often rendered almost unintelligible by specialists who ignore their interaction. On the other hand there is an equally serious danger in making too much of the connection between them. If they are all represented as mere phases of one common spirit of the age, their real distinctness is sacrificed to an empty and formal unity. To say that the mercantile system, the rise of standing armies, and the discovery of the differential calculus were all connected is true, but it tells us very little. To say that they were all expressions of the rise of rationalism or the modern spirit or some other such vague tendency tells us scarcely anything more, and may easily become an excuse for neglecting to show what each of them was in its own setting. The business of the historian is not merely to show that they were connected but how, and how far.

If the history of civilization is thus to carve reality at the joints, it will reject some famous theories which attempt to explain all historical phenomena in terms of a single principle. Of these the most widely prevalent at the present time is the economic interpretation of history, according to which the economic life of man, in whatever sense " economic " be understood, explains all the rest of his life. . . . In these chapters an attempt has been made to trace the connection of economic with other affairs. Both in these and in the later chapters, which deal with political events and the history of thought, of religion, and of the arts, it will be seen that new factors have to be taken into the reckoning which are not rooted in economic life. If this method is discordant with the economic interpretation, it is even more evidently fatal to the cruder theories which seek to explain the whole of history on grounds of climate or race.

It may be said that such a history is only a starting-point and not a final view of the matter, and that a full analysis of civilization ought to dig down to the depths of psychology and show how the constructive work of organized life is related to the fundamental desires and emotions of the

individual man. That may be so, but there are
ample reasons for not going down in the present
book to the sub-soil of folk-lore, superstition, the
half-conscious, and the irrational. These studies
require a different method, and they are not yet
in a condition which permits of a treatment other
than controversial. For the present purpose it is
sufficient that civilization in the narrow sense has
a history with its own clear limits.

G. N. CLARK, *The Seventeenth Century*, ix., x.

A New Science

IT would be premature at present to speculate as
to the number of motte and bailey castles which
can be connected with the centres of important
fees. The number is certainly considerable, but
the feudal geography of England is a new science,
and its elements have hardly been established as
yet.

F. M. STENTON, *The First Century of English Feudalism*
(1932), p. 198.

The " New " History

SINCE the days of Mommsen and Ranke, historians
have given their best energies to the " assemblage "
of raw materials—inscriptions, documents, and the
like—in " corpus "es and periodicals ; and, when
they have attempted to " work " these materials
" up " into " manufactured " or " semi-manu-
factured " articles, they have had recourse, once

again, to the Division of Labour and have produced synthetic histories like the several series of volumes now in course of publication by the Cambridge University Press. Such series are monuments of the laboriousness, the "factual" knowledge, the mechanical skill, and the organizing power of our society. They will take their rank with our stupendous tunnels and bridges and dams and liners and battleships and skyscrapers, and their editors will be remembered among the famous Western engineers. In invading the realm of historical thought, the Industrial System has given scope to great strategists and has set up marvellous trophies of victory. Yet, in a detached onlooker's mind, the doubt arises whether this conquest may not, after all, be a *tour de force* and the confidence of victory the delusion of a false analogy.

Some historical teachers of our day deliberately describe their "seminars" as "laboratories," and, perhaps less consciously but no less decidedly, restrict the term "original work" to denote the discovery or verification of some fact or facts not previously established. At the furthest, the term is extended to cover the interim reports upon such work which are contributed to learned journals or to synthetic histories. There is a strong tendency to depreciate works of historical literature which are created by single minds, and the depreciation becomes the more emphatic the nearer such works approximate to being "Universal Histories." For example, Mr. H. G. Wells' *The Outline of History* was received with unmistakable hostility by a number of historical specialists. They criticized severely the errors which they discovered at the points where the writer, in his long journey through Time and Space, happened to traverse their tiny allotments. They seemed not to realize that, in re-living the entire life of Mankind as a single imaginative experience, Mr. Wells was achieving something which they themselves would hardly have dared to attempt—something, perhaps, of which they had never conceived the possibility. In fact, the purpose and value of Mr. Wells' book seem to have been better appreciated by the general public than by the professional historians of the day.

.   .   .   .

These multiple tendencies can be summed up in a single formula : In the new age, the dominant note in the corporate consciousness of communities is a sense of being parts of some larger universe, whereas, in the age which is now over, the dominant note in their consciousness was an aspiration to be universes in themselves. This change of note indicates an unmistakable turn in a tide which, when it reached high-water mark about the year 1875, had been flowing steadily in one direction for four centuries. It may portend a return, in this respect, to the conditions of the preceding phase (the so-called " medieval " phase) of Western history, when the consciousness of the Western Society was dominated by institutions like the Papacy and the Holy Roman Empire which incorporated some aspect of its life as a whole, while kingdoms and city-states and fiefs and other local institutions were felt to be something parochial and subordinate. At any rate, that is the direction in which the tide seems to be flowing now—as far as it is possible to discern its direction so short a time after it has turned.

If this observation is correct, and if it is also true that historians cannot abstract their thoughts and feelings from the influence of the environment in which they live, then we may expect to witness in the near future a change in the outlook and activities of Western historians corresponding to the recent change in the general conditions of the Western Society. Just as, at the close of the age which we have left behind, the historians' work was brought into conformity with the Industrial System and their vision was caught and bounded by the idea of Nationality, so, in the new age upon which we have entered, they will probably find their intelligible field of study in some landscape where the horizon is not restricted to the boundaries of a single nationality, and will adapt their present method of work to mental operations on a larger scale.

A. J. TOYNBEE, *The Study of History*, I., pp. 3–5, 15

III

THE HISTORIAN AT WORK

Study well these books, Signor; for, believe
me, you will find that they will exhilarate and
improve your mind.

Don Quixote, c. 39.

III

THE HISTORIAN AT WORK

Advice to Historians

I SHALL never again enjoy the opportunity of speaking my thoughts to such an audience as this, and on so privileged an occasion a lecturer may well be tempted to bethink himself whether he knows of any neglected truth, any cardinal proposition, that might serve as his selected epigraph, as a last signal, perhaps even as a target. I am not thinking of those shining precepts which are the registered property of every school ; that is to say—Learn as much by writing as by reading ; be not content with the best book ; seek sidelights from the others ; have no favourites ; keep men and things apart ; guard against the prestige of great names ; see that your judgments are your own, and do not shrink from disagreement ; no trusting without testing ; be more severe to ideas than to actions ; do not overlook the strength of the bad cause, or the weakness of the good ; never be surprised by the crumbling of an idol or the disclosure of a skeleton ; judge talent at its best and character at its worst ; suspect power more than vice, and study problems in preference to periods; for instance: the derivation of Luther, the scientific influence of Bacon, the predecessors of Adam Smith, the medieval masters of Rousseau, the consistency of Burke, the identity of the first Whig. Most of this, I suppose, is undisputed, and calls for no enlargement. But the weight of opinion is against me when I exhort you never to debase the moral currency or to lower the standard of rectitude, but to try others by the final maxim that governs your own lives, and to suffer no man and no cause to escape the undying penalty which history has the power to inflict on wrong. The plea in extenuation of guilt and mitigation of punishment is perpetual. At every step we are met by arguments which go to excuse, to palliate, to confound right and wrong, and reduce the just man to the level of the reprobate.

LORD ACTON, *Lectures on Modern History*, pp. 23–24, 'Inaugural Lecture on the Study of History.'

Historical Method

THE main thing to learn is not the art of accumulating material, but the sublimer art of investigating it, of discerning truth from falsehood, and certainty from doubt. It is by solidity of criticism more than by the plenitude of erudition, that the study of history strengthens, and straightens, and extends the mind. And the accession of the critic in the place of the indefatigable compiler, of the artist in coloured narrative, the skilled limner of character, the persuasive advocate of good, or other, causes, amounts to a transfer of government, to a change of dynasty, in the historic realm. For the critic is one who, when he lights on an interesting statement, begins by suspecting it. He remains in suspense until he has subjected his authority to three operations. First, he asks whether he has read the passage as the author wrote it. For the transcriber and the editor, and the official or officious censor on the top of the editor, have played strange tricks, and have much to answer for. And if they are not to blame, it may turn out that the author wrote his book twice over, that you can discover the first jet, the progressive variations, things added, and things struck out. Next is the question where the writer got his information. If from a previous writer, it can be ascertained, and the inquiry has to be repeated. If from unpublished papers, they must be traced, and when the fountain-head is reached, or the track disappears, the question of veracity arises. The responsible writer's character, his position, antecedents, and probable motives have to be examined into ; and this is what, in a different and adapted sense of the word, may be called the higher criticism, in comparison with the servile and often mechanical work of pursuing statements to their root. For a historian has to be treated as a witness, and not believed unless his sincerity is established. The maxim that a man must be presumed to be innocent until his guilt is proved, was not made for him.

LORD ACTON, *On the Study of History*, pp. 15–16.

Archæology and History

WITH the Roman occupation the student of
Hampshire antiquities enters on the historic
period. He ceases to depend solely upon the
archæological evidence ; the narratives or the
allusions of ancient writers lend him their aid,
and he might, perhaps, be expected at this point
to commence a regular history. In reality he
cannot do that. Two facts, which are not always
adequately recognized, limit him to a more
humble, though not an easier task. The first of
these facts is to be found in the character of the
Roman Empire, of which Britain formed a province. Alike in its vast extent and its complex
organization, that Empire was constituted on a
scale which reduces details to insignificance. Its
history is one of great development slowly ad-
vancing among the populations of three continents;
we do not meet in it that continuous individual
life, that rapid succession of incidents and quick
growth of tendencies which mark the cities of
ancient Greece or the little nations of modern
Europe. Single men, local occurrences, are the
least important items in the Roman imperial
annals, and the fortunes of single provinces disappear beside the great movement of the whole mass.
We can describe the characteristics of each province, its populousness, its degree of civilization,
its mineral or agricultural or commercial wealth,
and we can string together into a rough sketch a
few events connected with it. But we cannot
write a real history of it.

A second fact imposes an equally serious limitation. When the Romans ruled our island, it was not divided into its present countries nor into any districts geographically identical with them. Neither the boundaries of the Celtic tribes, nor those of the Roman administrative areas, so far as we know them, agree with existing county boundaries. The student of Roman remains found in any one county has to deal with a division of land which for his purpose is accidental and arbitrary. The phrase Roman Hampshire may be convenient, but, strictly speaking, it is a contradiction in terms. The limits of Hampshire coincide neither with the limits of the Belgae, Aliebates, and other Celtic tribes inhabiting it, not with any divisions set up by the Romans. For our present purpose it is a meaningless area with no unity. We can describe it, but we cannot write a history of it.

These two facts make it desirable to diverge a little from the plan followed by most county historians in dealing with the Roman antiquities of the county described. Hitherto, it has been customary to give a narrative of the chief events recorded by ancient writers as having occurred in Britain, and to point out which of these events took place, or may be imagined to have taken place, within the county. The result is always to give an impression that somehow the county had in Roman times some sort of local individuality and local history. We shall here adopt a different plan, suggested by the recent developments of archæological research. Utilizing the abundant archæological evidence, which is now far better known and appreciated than it was a hundred or two hundred years ago, we shall try first to sketch briefly the general character of the Roman province of Britain, its military, social, and economic features. We shall then point out in some detail how far the antiquities of Hampshire illustrate this general sketch ; that is, how far the district now called Hampshire was an ordinary and average bit of Roman Britain.

The Roman occupation commenced in A.D. 43. At first its progress was rapid. Within three or four years the Romans overran all the south and midlands as far as Exeter, Shrewsbury, and Lincoln ; part was annexed, part left to " protected " native princes. Then came a pause ; some thirty years were spent in reducing the hill tribes of Wales and Yorkshire, and during this period the " protected " principalities were gradually absorbed. About A.D. 80 the advance into Scotland was attempted : in 124 Hadrian built his Wall from Newcastle to Carlisle, and thereafter the Roman frontier was sometimes to the north, never to the south of this line. The " province " thus gained fell practically, though not officially, into two marked divisions, which coincide roughly with the lowlands occupied in the first years of the conquest and the hills which were tamed later. The former were the districts of settled civil life. The troops appear to have been very soon withdrawn from them, and with a few definite exceptions, there was probably not a fort or fortress or military post throughout this part of our island. On the other hand, the Welsh and northern hills formed a purely military district, with forts and fortresses and roads, but with no towns or ordinary civilian life. It was the Roman practice, at least in the European provinces of the Empire, to mass the troops almost exclusively along the frontiers, and Britain was no exception. The army which garrisoned this military district was perhaps forty thousand men. It ranked as one of the chief among provincial armies, and constituted the most important element in Roman Britain.

With the military district, however, we are not now concerned. For our present purpose it suffices to note its existence, in order to explain why the traces of military occupation are rare in Hampshire. But we may pause to examine the chief features of the non-military districts within which the area of Hampshire is included. These features are not sensational. Britain was a small province, remote from Rome, and by no means wealthy. It did not reach the higher developments of city life, of culture, or of commerce, which we meet in more favoured lands—Gaul or Spain or Africa. Nevertheless, it had a character of its own.

In the first place, Britain, like all the provinces of the western empire, became Romanized. Perhaps it became Romanized later and less perfectly than these, but in the end the Britons adopted generally the Roman speech and civilization, and in our island, as in all western Europe, the difference between Roman and provincial practically vanished. When the Roman rule in Britain ended (about A.D. 410), the so-called departure of the Romans did not mean what the end of English rule in India or French rule in Algeria would mean. It was not an emigration of alien officials, soldiers, and traders. It meant rather what the severance of New Zealand or Australia from England would mean to-day : it was more administrative than racial. Probably the country folk in the remoter parts of Britain continued to speak Celtic during the Roman period : this much we may infer from continental analogies and from the revival of Celtic in the sixth century. But the townspeople and the educated seem to have used Latin, and on the side of material civilization the Roman element reigns supreme. Before the Roman period there was a late Celtic art of considerable merit, best known for its metal work and earthenware, and distinguished for its fantastic use of plant and animal forms, its employment of the " returning spiral," and its enamelling. This art and the culture which went with it vanished before the Roman. In a few places, as in the New Forest, its products survived as local curiosities ; in general it met the fate of every picturesque but semi-civilized art when confronted by an organized coherent culture. Almost every feature in Romano-British life was Roman. The commonest good pottery, the so-called Samian, or Terra Sigillata, was copied directly from an Italian original, and shows no trace of Celtic influences ; it was indeed principally imported from Gaul. The mosaic pavements and painted stuccoes which adorned the houses, the hypocausts which warmed them, and the bathrooms which increased their luxury, were equally borrowed from Italy. Nor were these features confined to the mansions of the wealthy. Samian bowls and coarsely-coloured plaster and makeshift hypocausts occur even in the cottages of outlying hamlets. The material civilization of Roman Britain comprised few elements of splendour or magnificence, but it was definitely and decisively Roman.

Agreeably to this general character of the province, we find town life in it, but the highest form of town life known to the Romans is naturally rare. The *coloniae* and *municipia*, the privileged municipalities with constitutions on the Italian model, which mark the supreme development of Roman political civilization in the provinces, were not common in Britain. We know only of five. Colchester, Lincoln, Gloucester, and York were *coloniae*, Verulam probably a *municipium*, and, despite their legal rank, none of these could count among the greater cities of the Empire. Four of them probably owe their existence, not to any development of Britain, but to the need of providing for " time-expired " soldiers discharged from the army.

On the other hand, many smaller towns reached some degree of municipal life. Originally (as it seems) Celtic tribal centres, they grew into towns, just as the tribal centres of northern Gaul grew into towns, under the influence of Roman civilization. They were mostly small, but their sizes varied widely—from hardly twenty to more than two hundred acres. Strong walls protected them from external assault ; inside, at least in the larger towns, a prison built on the Roman plan, provided accommodation for magistrates, traders, and idlers. What was the legal status of such a town, what town council or police it had, we do not know, but we can hardly doubt that some sort of town life existed there. Hampshire contains two instances of such towns—Silchester and Winchester; others are Canterbury and Rochester, Dorchester and Exeter, Cirencester, Leicester, and, far in the north, Aldborough in the Vale of York.

Outside these towns the country seems to have been principally divided up into estates, usually called " villas," and in this respect again Britain resembles northern Gaul. The " villa " was the property of a large landowner who lived in the " great house," if there was one, cultivated the land immediately round it (the demesne) by his slaves, and let the rest to half-serf colonies. The " villa " system, in fact, was the origin of the mediæval manorial system, and on the Continent (though not in our island) the development of the one into the other can be traced continuously. The estates doubtless varied in size as much as estates in all ages and countries. In Gaul they are said sometimes to have included eight or ten thousand acres, but we have no means of judging in Britain. They formed, for the most part, sheep runs and corn land, and supplied the cloth and wheat which are occasionally mentioned by ancient writers as products of the province during the later Imperial period. The landowners may have been to some extent immigrant Italians, but it can hardly be doubted that, as in Gaul, they were mostly the Romanized upper classes of the natives. The common assertion that they were Roman officers or officials may be set aside as rarely, if ever, correct.

The houses of these landowners deserve a word of notice, for they do not in the least resemble the houses of ancient Rome or Pompeii. They belong, principally, to two kindred types, which occur only in Britain and in northern Gaul. One of these types is simpler than the other : it shows a straight row or range of rooms with a passage along them, and it has been denominated the Corridor type. The other shows three such rows of rooms with corridors set round three sides of a tolerably large, open, rectangular yard, and it has been denominated the Courtyard type. Both kinds occur indifferently in towns and in the country, but in the country they are naturally supplemented by outbuildings, barns, and cottages. The corridor houses are generally the smaller of the two kinds : some of them measure hardly more than forty to sixty feet, while in the larger courtyard houses the yards alone may be three times that size. These dimensions refer only to the ground-floors, but upper stories were probably rare, and we can therefore guess reasonably at the total accommodation. The origin of these two types of house is uncertain. They are unquestionably distinct from anything Italian. Probably they were in the first instance rural. As a glance at the plan of Silchester will show, neither the Courtyard houses nor the Corridor houses fit, like proper town houses, into streets : they are county houses loosely conglomerated, with much garden space between. They occur in the specially Celtic districts of Britain and northern Gaul, and we may be tempted to suppose them Celtic. The Celts in these countries had in

Cæsar's time a definite style (or styles) of house building. Perhaps our two types are the descendants of what Cæsar saw, modified by Roman additions of mosaic and fresco and hypocaust and bathroom, but substantially indigenous.

The peasantry who worked on these estates, or were otherwise occupied in the country, lived in rude hamlets, sometimes in pit dwellings, sometimes in huts, with few circumstances of comfort or pleasure. Their civilization, however, as we have said, was purely Roman in all such matters as the better objects in common use or the warming and decoration of the houses. Even among the country folk the Late Celtic art appears mainly to have vanished.

F. HAVERFIELD, *Victoria County History, Hampshire*, I., pp. 265–70.

History as Literature

WHEN at the beginning of 1560 there was a new Pope, pledged to convoke the Council for a third time and to stem and repel the tide of heresy, the latest disaster that met his eye was no mere relapse of England followed by a lapse of Scotland ; for what was shaping itself in the northern seas already looked ominously like a Protestant Great Britain. Two small Catholic Powers traditionally at war with each other, the one a satellite of the Habsburg luminary, the other a satellite of France, seemed to be fusing themselves in one Power that might be very great :

great perhaps for good, but more probably for evil. "Earnest embracing of religion," wrote a Scottish to an English statesman, "will join us straitly together." The religion that William Maitland meant when he sent these words to Sir William Cecil was not the religion of Pius IV. and the General Council.

Suddenly all far-sighted eyes had turned to a backward country. Eyes at home and eyes at Geneva were fixed on Scotland, and, the further they could peer into the future, the more eager must have been their gaze. And still we look intently at that wonderful scene, the Scotland of Mary Stewart and John Knox : not merely because it is such glorious tragedy, but also because it is such modern history. The fate of the Protestant Reformation was being decided, and the creed of unborn millions in undiscovered lands was being determined. This we see—all too plainly perhaps—if we read the books that year by year men still are writing of Queen Mary and her surroundings. The patient analysis of those love letters in the casket may yet be perturbed by thoughts about religion. Nor is the religious the only interest. A new nation, a British nation, was in the making.

We offer no excuse for having as yet said little of Scotland. Called upon to play for some years a foremost part in the great drama, her entry upon the stage of modern history is late and sudden. In such phrases there must indeed be some untruth, for history is not drama. The annals of Scotland may be so written that the story will be continuous enough. We may see the explosion of 1559 as the effect of causes that had long been at work. We might chronicle the remote beginnings of heresy and the first glimmers of the New Learning. All those signs of the times that we have seen elsewhere in capital letters we might see here in minuscule. Also, it would not escape us that, though in the days of Luther and Calvin resistance to the English and their obstinately impolitic claim of suzerainty still seemed the vital thread of Scottish national existence, inherited enmity was being enfeebled, partly by the multiplying perfidies of venal nobles and the increasing wealth of their paymasters, and partly also by the accumulating proofs that in the new age a Scotland which lived only to help France and hamper England would herself be a poor little Power among the nations : doomed, not only to occasional Floddens and Pinkies, but to continuous misery, anarchy, and obscurity.

All this deserves, and finds, full treatment at the hands of the historians of Scotland. They will also sufficiently warn us that the events of 1560 leave a great deal unchanged. Faith may be changed ; works are much what they were, especially the works of the magnates. The blood-feud is no less a blood-feud because one family calls itself Catholic and another calls itself Protestant. The " band " is no less a " band " because it is styled a " Covenant " and makes free with holy names. A King shall be kidnapped and a King shall be murdered, as of old—it is the custom of the country. What is new is that far-sighted men all Europe over, not only at London and at Paris but at Rome and at Geneva, should take interest in these barbarous deeds, this customary turmoil.

Continuity there had been and to spare. In that mournful procession of the five Jameses there is no break (1406–1542). The last of them is engaged in the old task, and failing as his forebears failed. It is picturesque; sometimes it is heroic; often it is pathetic; but it is never modern. Modern history sees it as a funeral procession burying a dead time, and we are silent while it passes. In a few sentences we make our way towards the momentous years.

. . . .

In controversy with the Puritans the Elizabethan religion gradually assumed an air of moderation which had hardly belonged to it from the first; it looked like a compromise between an old faith and a new. It is true that from the beginning of her reign Elizabeth distrusted Calvin; and when she swore that she never read his books she may have sworn the truth. That blast of the trumpet had repelled her. Not only had " the regiment of women " been attacked, but Knox and Goodman had advocated a divine right of rebellion against idolatrous Princes. Calvin might protest his innocence; but still this dangerous stuff came from his Geneva. Afterwards, however, he took an opportunity of being serviceable to the Queen in the matter of a book which spoke ill of her father and mother. Then a pretty message went to him and he was bidden to feel assured of her favour (September 18, 1561). Moreover, in German history Elizabeth appears as espousing the cause of oppressed Calvinists

against the oppressing Lutherans. Still as time
went on, when the Huguenots, as she said, had
broken faith with her about Havre and Calais,
and the attack on "her officers," the Bishops,
was being made in the name of the Genevan
discipline, her dislike of Geneva, its works, and
its ways, steadily grew. Though in the region of
pure theology Calvin's influence increased apace
in England and Scotland after his death, and
Whitgift, the stern repressor of the Puritans, was
a remorseless predestinarian, still the Bishops saw,
albeit with regret, that they had two frontiers to
defend, and that they could not devote all their
energy to the confutation of the Louvainists.

Then some severed, or half-severed, bonds were
spliced. Parker was a lover of history, and it was
pleasant to sit in the chair of Augustine, seeing
to editions of Ælfric's Homilies and the Chronicles
of Matthew Paris. But the work was slowly done,
and foreigners took a good share in it. Hadrian
Saravia, who defended English episcopacy against
Beza, was a refugee, half Spaniard, half Fleming.
Pierre Baron of Cambridge, who headed a movement against Calvin's doctrine of the divine
decrees, was another Frenchman, another pupil
of the law-school of Bourges. And it is to be
remembered that at Elizabeth's accession the
Genevan was not the only model for a radically
Reformed Church. The fame of Zwingli's Zurich
had hardly yet been eclipsed, and for many years
the relation between the Anglican and Tigurine
Churches was close and cordial. A better example
of a purely spiritual power could hardly be found
than the influence that was exercised in England

by Zwingli's successor, Henry Bullinger. Bishops and Puritans argue their causes before him as if he were the judge. So late as 1586 English clergymen are required to peruse his immortal *Decades*. There was some gratitude in the case. A silver cup with verses on it had spoken Elizabeth's thanks for the hospitality that he had shown to Englishmen. But that was not all; he sympathized with Elizabeth and her Bishops and her Erastianism. He condemned "the English fool" who broke the peace of the Palatinate by a demand for the Genevan discipline. When the cry was that the congregation should elect its minister, the Puritan could be told how in an admirably reformed republic Protestant pastors were still chosen by patrons who might be papists, even by a Bishop of Constance who might be the Pope's own nephew and a Cardinal to boot, for a Christian magistracy would see that this patronage was not abused. And then when the bad day came and the Pope hurled his thunderbolt, it was to Bullinger that the English Bishops looked for a learned defence of their Queen and their creed. Modestly, but willingly, he undertook the task: none the less willingly, perhaps, because Pius V had seen fit to couple Elizabeth's name with Calvin's, and this was a controversialist's trick which Zurich could expose. Bullinger knew all the Puritan woes and did not like surplices; he knew and much disliked the "semi-popery" of Lutheran Germany; but in his eyes the Church of England was no half-way house. As to Elizabeth, he saw her as no lukewarm friend of true religion, but as a virgin-queen beloved of God,

153

whose wisdom and clemency, whose felicity and dexterity were a marvel and a model for all Christian Princes (March 12, 1572).

The felicity and dexterity are not to be denied. The Elizabethan religion which satisfied Bullinger was satisfying many other people also ; for (to say nothing of intrinsic merits or defects) it appeared as part and parcel of a general amelioration. It was allied with honest money, cheap and capable government, national independence, and a reviving national pride. The long Terror was overpast, at least for a while ; the flow of noble blood was stayed ; the axe rusted at the Tower. The long Elizabethan peace was beginning (1563), while France was ravaged by civil war, and while more than half the Scots looked to the English Queen as the defender of their faith. One Spaniard complains that these heretics have not their due share of troubles (November, 1562) ; another, that they are waxing fat upon the spoil of the Indies (August, 1565). The England into which Francis Bacon was born in 1561 and William Shakespeare in 1564 was already unlike the England that was ruled by the Queen of Spain.

F. W. MAITLAND, " The Anglican Settlement and the Scottish Reformation " (*Cambridge Modern History*, II., ch. xvi., pp. 550–51, 597–98).

The Working Historian

(a)

A NEW and happy *et cætera* was introduced into the royal style and seemed to hint, without naming, a Headship of the Church.

F. W. MAITLAND, *Cambridge Modern History*, II., 564.

(b)

FOR nearly two hundred and fifty years the solemn style and title of the king or queen of this country ended with the words " and so forth " or in Latin *et cætera*. On the first day of the nineteenth century a change was made. Queen Victoria's grandfather became king of a " United Kingdom " of Great Britain and Ireland. He ceased to be King of France. He also ceased to be " and so forth."

Had this phrase always been meaningless ? I venture to suggest that it had its origin in a happy thought, a stroke of genius.

If we look at the book to which we naturally turn when we would study the styles and titles of our English kings, if we look at Sir Thomas Hardy's Introduction to the Charter Rolls, we shall observe that the first sovereign who bears an " &c " is Queen Elizabeth. Now let us for a moment place ourselves in the first days of her reign. Shall we not be eager to know what this new queen will call herself, for will not her style be a presage of her policy ? No doubt she is by the Grace of God of England, France, and Ireland Queen. No doubt she is Defender of the Faith, though we cannot be sure what faith she will defend. But is that all? Is she or is she not Supreme Head upon earth of the Church of England and Ireland?

The full difficulty of the question which this young lady had to face so soon as she was safely queen may not be justly appreciated by our modern minds. We say, perhaps, that acts of parliament had bestowed a certain title, and had since been repealed by other acts of parliament. But to this bald statement we must make two additions. In the first place, one at least of the Henrician statutes had declared that the headship of the Church was annexed to the kingship by a bond stronger and holier than any act of parliament: to wit, by the very word of God. In the second place, one of the Marian statutes had rushed to the opposite limit. It had in effect declared that Henry's ecclesiastical supremacy had all along been a nullity. It had indeed excused Queen Mary's temporary assumption of a title that was not rightfully hers, and documents in which the obnoxious phrase occurred were not for that reason to be invalid; but it applauded Mary for having seen the error of her ways, and having of her own motion rejected a title which no parliament could lawfully confer.

It was a difficult problem. On both sides there were men with extreme opinions, who, however, agreed in holding that the solution of the question was not to be found in any earthly statute book.

. . . .

Then a happy thought occurs. Let her highness
etceterate herself. This will leave her hands free,
and then afterwards she can explain the etceteration as occasion shall require. Suppose that
sooner or later she must submit to the pope, she
can still say that she has done no wrong. She
can plead that, at least in some of his documents,
King Philip, the Catholic King, etceterates himself. There are always, so it might be said, some
odds and ends that might conveniently be packed
up in " and so forth." What of the Channel
Islands, for example? They are not parts of
England, and they are hardly parts of France.
Besides, even Paul IV. would be insaner than we
think him, if, when securing so grand a prize as
England, he boggled over an &c. And then, on
the other hand, if her grace finds it advisable, as
perhaps it will be, to declare that the Marian
statutes are null, she cannot be reproached with
having been so bad as her sister, for we shall say
that no reasonable man, considering all that has
happened, can have doubted that the " &c "
signified that portion of King Henry's title and
King Edward's title which, for the sake of brevity,
was not written in full. Lastly, suppose that the
parliament which is now to be summoned is
willing to go great lengths in an Erastian, and
Protestant direction, no harm will have been done.
Indeed, hereafter the queen's highness in her
exercise of her ecclesiastical supremacy may find
it advisable to assert that this supremacy was in
being before any parliament recognized its existence, and therefore is not to be controlled even
by the estates of the realm. Therefore, let her be

" defender of the faith, and so forth." He who
knows what faith is " the " faith will be able to
make a good guess touching the import of " and
so forth."

. . . .

Now let us discover, if we can, the moment of
time at which the etceteration began. So to do is
the more important because I am not in a position
to contend that this addition to the royal style is
to be found in every place in which, if my theory
be true, it ought to occur. In particular, any one
who relied only on the officially printed volumes
of statutes might infer that the change took place
before the parliament of 1563, but after the parliament of 1559. On the other hand, we may see the
little syllable on a writ of January 21, 1559 which
prorogued parliament from the 23rd to the 25th
of that month. Occasionally a clerk will make a
slip, an omissive slip : especially by leaving un-
modified an old formula which he ought to modify.
So let us look at the very first document in which
Queen Elizabeth announced her royal will and
pleasure. In Humfrey Dyson's collection at the
British Museum lies the proclamation " imprynted
at London by Richard Jugge," which tells us how
it hath pleased Almighty God to call to His mercy
out of this mortal life, to our great grief, " our
deerest suster of noble memory," and how the
kingdoms of England, France, and Ireland, " with
all maner titles and rights thereunto in any wise
apperteyning," have come to Us, " Elizabeth, by
the grace of God Queene of Englande Fraunce
and Ireland defendour of the fayth, &c."

A little later Mary's body was borne to the

grave, and there was heraldic display, of which an apparently official account is extant. Heralds are bound to be careful of titles. The late queen had a lengthy title, but it must be recited at full length. Then, when the dirge has been chanted and the crowd is questioning whether many more dirges will be chanted in England, comes the demand for a loyal shout for a new queen, whose title is brief, but who is something that her sister was not ; for she is &c.

Then we know that parliament had hardly assembled (25 January) before the Commons appointed (30 January) a committee to consider the validity of the summons which had called them together, and of the writs by virtue whereof some of Mary's last parliaments were holden. The committee reported (3 February) that the omission of the words *Supremum Caput* was no cause of nullity. I should suppose that Elizabeth's ministers had by this time decided—and surely it was a wise decision—that whatever ecclesiastical changes were to be made should be made in a straightforward manner by repeal, and should not be attempted by means of a theory which Roman Catholics and Calvinists would accuse of blasphemy and the plain man would charge with chicane. It may be, therefore, that they never had to rely on their " &c " ; but some of us would gladly have been present at the deliberations of that committee.

Some years later certain English members of the Roman Church were consulting some high authority—not the Pope himself, but some high authority—touching the course of conduct that

they ought to pursue towards a queen whom
Pius V. had denounced as excommunicate and
deposed. . . . These scrupulous persons desire
to know whether Elizabeth may be called Queen
of England, and, if so, whether the " &c " may be
added. . . . If, then, we see significance in this
" &c," we are only seeing what was seen by some
at least of Elizabeth's subjects, and the brain
to which *illa particula* occurred seems to deserve
credit for its ingenuity. Catholic and Calvinist
can say that this is a *vox indifferens* common in
regal styles. On the other hand, the champions
of a divinely instituted cæsaro-papalism will observe that all Elizabeth's possible titles, except
one, have been expressly named.

For all this we might fear that we were making
much ado about nothing, and discovering deep
policy in some clerk's flourish, were it not for a
piece of evidence that remains to be mentioned.
At the Record Office is preserved a paper on which
Cecil has scribbled memoranda. It is ascribed to
Nov. 18, 1558, the second day of Elizabeth's
reign. Apparently the secretary is taking his
mistress' pleasure about a great variety of matters,
and, as he does so, he jots down notes which will
aid his memory. Ambassadors must be sent to
foreign princes ; a new great seal must be en-
graved ; a preacher must be selected to fill the
pulpit at Paul's Cross next Sunday. Then, among
these notes—which should be photographed, for
no print could represent them—we find the
following :

A commission to make out wrythes for y^e parlement
touchyng &c. in y^e style of wryttes.

This seems to me proof positive that " &c. in the style of writs " was the outcome, not of chance but of deliberation that took place at the first moment of the reign in the highest of high quarters.

So we might expand the symbol thus :

&c. = and (if future events shall so decide, but not further or otherwise) of the Church of England and also of Ireland upon earth the Supreme Head.

> F. W. MAITLAND, *Collected Papers*, III., 157–65;
> *Elizabethan Gleanings*, i., " Defender of the Faith,
> and so forth."

A Portrait

THE trial was fixed for December 1. Winchester, whom Knox designates as " the crafty fox, Shebna," and describes as one of Somerset's most active foes, was appointed lord high steward to preside over the court. Of the twenty-six peers summoned to sit, Winchester, Northumberland, Suffolk, Northampton, and Pembroke were the most conspicuous. They were challenged as being parties to the case, but a peer was supposed to be immune from the prejudices of ordinary jurymen and might not legally be challenged on the score of partiality. In the darkness of a December morning, between five and six o'clock, Somerset was brought by water from the Tower to Westminster Hall, and strict injunctions were given that the people should remain indoors. The court contained no partisan of Somerset, but even so, it could not be persuaded to believe the charge of treason. As a compromise between acquittal and condemnation for treason, the prisoner was pronounced guilty of felony ; and Northumberland and Winchester made a merit of their mercy in withholding a penalty which they could not induce the court to inflict. Many peers expected that the death sentence would be commuted for imprisonment ; and the people, on seeing Somerset taken back to the Tower, with the axe averted, cast off their usual stony indifference, threw up their caps, and raised shouts which rolled up Whitehall and were heard in Long Acre fields. Some thought the duke was acquitted, others hoped for his pardon, and cried " God save him " all the way back to the Tower.

The lords, says the chronicler, were astounded at this demonstration ; and if Northumberland had ever thought of mercy, this indication of the strength of popular feeling in Somerset's favour dispelled it ; he was not likely to pardon a dangerous rival. For seven weeks Somerset lay under sentence of death, consoling himself by inditing pious reflections. His execution was precipitated by the necessity for summoning parliament. It was called for January 23, and would assuredly exert itself on Somerset's behalf. On the 18th Edward drew up a memorandum of business for the privy council ; one of the items was " the matter for the Duke of Somerset's confederates to be considered as apperteineth to our surety and quietness of our realm, that by their punishment example may be shewed to others." Before this memorandum was submitted to the board, the wording had been altered by Edward himself or some one else so as to run, " The matter for the Duke of Somerset *and his* confederates . . . that by their punishment *and execution*," etc. The first version was an instruction to the Council to take measures for the trial of Fane, Partridge, Stanhope, and others who had not yet been put on their defence ; the second was an order to arrange for Somerset's execution, and we shall see that by a similar alteration of Edward's words, another of Northumberland's schemes was brought to pass later on.

At eight in the morning of the 22nd, " when hardly any person suspected such an event," Somerset was brought out on to the scaffold on Tower Hill ; he made no confession of the crimes with which he was charged, and the crowd received with approving cries his protests of devotion to the King and commonwealth. A sudden explosion interrupted his speech, and a panic ensued ; Somerset might have escaped in the confusion, and was censured for lack of spirit in not making the attempt.

The resignation and dignity of his behaviour add to the difficulty of summing up the protector's strangely incoherent character. His uniform success as a military commander is in sharp contrast with the visionary nature of his political aims ; and the greed with which he seized on the spoils of the Church seems to belie the generosity with which he treated his tenants. The hauteur he displayed towards colleagues conflicts with the humility with which he accepted his fate ; and the obstinacy with which he championed the poor sets off the facility with which he abandoned his brother. He had no taste nor gift for intrigue himself, but he was pliant in the hands of subtler schemers. Of his bravery, of his personal morality, and of the sincerity of his religious professions there can be no doubt, though his lack of zeal caused many Protestants to compare him unfavourably with Warwick. He did not betray his friends or shirk responsibility, and he was somewhat lost in the devious ways of the statecraft of his age. " He was endowed and enriched with the most excellent gifts of God both in body and in mind," wrote no friendly critic on his execution ; while another exclaimed, " And this is the end of an ambitious heart and insatiable mind." He was greedy of wealth and grasped at authority. But he pursued power for something more than its own sake and private advantage. His ideas were large and generous : he sought the union of England and Scotland, the advancement of liberty, the destruction of social injustice. As a statesman he was bankrupt without guile ; but his quick sympathies touched the heart of the people ; and it was no slight honour to be remembered as " the good duke " by that generation of Machiavelli.

A. F. POLLARD, *History of England, 1547–1603*, pp. 63–5.

The Scientific Historian

THOUGH Dr. Liebermann has still something in store for us in the way of notes, index, glossary, and the like, the time has already come when we may rejoice in the possession of a really good edition of the oldest English laws, an edition which will bear comparison with the very best work that has hitherto been done upon any historical materials of a similar kind. That this task should have been performed by a German scholar at the instance of a German academy, and with the support of a German trust fund, may not be what we in England should have liked best, but must not detract from the warmth of our welcome and our praise. If Englishmen cannot or will not do these things, they can at least rejoice that others can and will.

.   .   .   .

On the present occasion we will say but little of what has been done for the Anglo-Saxon laws, properly so called, for, as already said, some notes are yet to come. But already we have a translation of a very excellent kind—a translation from which even those who have but a slight acquaintance with the Old English tongue may gather both what a laconic legislator has said, and also what he has meant to an editor skilled in the early history of Teutonic law. We shall run no risk in saying that by this new version all older versions are superseded. As to the text, we do not like to speak of finality, but have great difficulty in imagining what more could have been done. In particular, students of language will, so we think, be hard to please if Dr. Liebermann has not given them material enough. Rejecting less exhaustive methods, he has printed in parallel columns the texts that are given by all the leading manuscripts. We open the book ; we see alongside each other three different English texts of the laws of Cnut and three different Latin versions of the same, while the new German translation fills the bottom of the page. It looks like the full score of an opera, and some time must be spent before we can master the manifold typographical devices which have been invented to save time and space. At first sight the editor seems to have a rooted objection to printing six consecutive words without a change of type ; and the natural man sighs for the simplicity of a pianoforte arrangement. But unquestionably all this elaborate technique, which must have taxed to their uttermost the resources of a great printing house, will be highly valued by philologists. Want of imagination has been a common fault in editors. A little difference in spelling, for example, seems to you too trivial for notice. A few years go by ; science strides forward ; you can be accused of jumbling two dialects together ; and then your work must be done over again. Never, it is rightly said, is a long day ; but we fancy that a long day will pass before Dr. Liebermann is charged with insufficiently minding his p's and q's. It would be admitted on all hands nowadays that the oldest monuments of the English language deserve as much care as an English, or any other, editor would ungrudgingly spend upon the most worthless scrap of classical Greek ; but we fear that we have been slow to take this truth to heart. A characteristic example occurs on Dr. Liebermann's first page. There is a word, now partly illegible, in the only medieval manuscript that gives the very earliest of all the laws. The English editor can only tell us of a guess. It struck Dr. Liebermann that what cannot be read now could perhaps be read in the sixteenth century by one of those antiquarian worthies who sometimes copied the more accurately, because they hardly aspired to understand what they were copying. And so a very "secondary source," Francis Tate's transcript of a manuscript that is still in our hands, solves the difficulty. Why did not we think of it?

.　　.　　.　　.　　.　　.　　.

Keen criticism of literary style is one of the tools in Dr. Liebermann's workshop. It is a highly useful weapon when anonymous products are to be dated or a forger is to be confronted with his handiwork, and yet we fancy that it will be almost news to many Englishmen that this weapon can be used not only—no one would doubt that—where literary style is reasonably good, but also, and with even greater effect, where style is abominably bad. As a relic of the old belief " that all the Middle Ages lived at the same time," there remains, we will not say a belief, but a disposition to think that all " low " Latin is equally low. Really, however, the style of these *Leges Henrici* is as distinctive as style could be : marvellously different from the glib Latinity of Lanfranc and his scholars. It is a highly distinctive compound of the worst sort of windy rhetoric and the mere dog-Latin of a man who is thinking in French about Anglo-Saxon technicalities. There is a repellent preface to one of his works. We fear that an English editor would have thought that he had done enough for

the sorry stuff when he had complained of its
turgidity. Not so Dr. Liebermann. The miser-
able man is not allowed to finish his first sentence
before the detective has found a clue. " Did
you say ' nullis aduersitatum liuoribus obatrescit ? '
Pardon me, but that is a Firmicianism. You
have come under the influence of the astrologer,
Julius Firmicus Maternus ; and that is another
link between you and Archbishop Gerard, who,
to the scandal of all right-thinking Christians,
died—at least, so the High Church people said—
with this necromancer's book under his pillow."

F. W. MAITLAND,
Collected Papers, III., pp. 447, 464–66, 471–72.

Narrative

So ended the Third of June, which sealed the
fate of Rome. On the same day, four miles to
the north, a less important operation had taken
place on the upper reaches of the Tiber, across
which the French had secured a passage by
capturing the Ponte Molle, in face of the *Reduci*
and the Roman Legion. But far the greater part
of Oudinot's army of 20,000 men—seven out of
nine regiments—had been concentrated in or near
the Pamfili grounds, ready to feed the battle at
the Corsini. It is doubtful whether more than
6,000 Italians in all were under Garibaldi's orders,
and these had not been together in force, but had
been coming up, one regiment after another, all
through the day : the Italian Legion was more
than half spent before the Bersaglieri arrived, and

the Bersaglieri before the Regiment *Unione* came on the scene. If we remember how enormous was the force of French regulars inside the fortress of the Pamfili-Corsini grounds, protected by a high wall on both flanks, the complaint made by some critics that Garibaldi did not attack the flank of the French position will appear of doubtful validity. Indeed, Dandolo has accused him of exactly the opposite fault, declaring that he wasted his slender forces by movements of his left flank, " skirmishing uselessly among the vineyards "— an accusation equally wide of the mark if it refers to the operations which resulted in the secure occupation of the Casa Giacometti, essential not only for the maintenance of the Vascello, but for the proper preparation and support of any attack on the Corsini. The unprepared frontal attack *en masse* by the Bersaglieri, which Dandolo believed would have been certainly successful, was in fact actually tried with a third part of the regiment in one charge, and would probably in so confined a space have had no better result with the whole. Those who complained that Garibaldi should have " entrenched " himself in the positions the moment after their capture, forget that on the Corsini hill the Italians that day had neither respite, time, nor materials for digging. The entrenchment ought to have been done by Roselli during the peaceful month of May.

But Garibaldi's mistakes on this day are bad enough, when all unjust censure has been put aside. Once, at least, we know that he threw a body of twenty men, unsupported, at the villa, and he is accused in general terms of having committed the same kind of folly several times. It is, however, clear that the principal attacks were made by large masses of men, and the proper criticism on the first attack by the Bersaglieri is not so much that the storming party was too small, but that the way had not been prepared by a sufficiently prolonged cannonade and musketry fire, such as afterwards drove the French from the villa. So, too, Masina's Lancers —whose lives Garibaldi is sometimes said to have thrown away in a wild-goose chase—took the villa by an attack admirably timed at the moment when the French defence was weak, and held it until the immediate arrival of the infantry. Unfortunately, at that late hour of the day, the discipline, though not the courage, of the spent regiments was giving way, and the hill could not be held by a courageous mob against the ordered attack of superior forces. No doubt there was a want of system and combination both in Garibaldi's methods of attack and in the support of the positions when captured. But it may be doubted whether the force which he had under him could, under any generalship in the world, have been sufficient, not only to capture (as it did several times in the day), but to hold the narrow Corsini line, against the concentrated fire and attack of the French army, drawn out in battle array in the broader Pamfili grounds.

Both sides fought with heroic courage, and each recognized the qualities of the enemy. But they did not love each other the better for that, and the trickery by which the positions had first been won sank deep into the Italian mind. " I find the wounded men in the hospital," wrote Margaret Fuller, " in a transport of indignation. The French soldiers fought so furiously that they think them false as their General, and cannot endure the remembrance of their visits, during the armistice, and talk of brotherhood." The anger of the Italians was more fierce than on April 30 ; some French prisoners were massacred on the scene of battle immediately after their surrender, and others were insulted on their way into Rome.

The Italians estimated their killed and wounded sometimes at 1,000, sometimes at 900, sometimes at 500 men and 50 officers. All fell in a space about 600 paces long by 300 wide, outside the Porta San Pancrazio. The French officially announced their loss at 250 men and 14 officers, which is the lowest estimate.

Of the killed and wounded, some 30 officers and 200 men belonged to Garibaldi's own Italian Legion. Hoffstetter, who was attached to the Bersaglieri of Manara, and became an historian of their prowess on this day, admitted that the Italian Legion had won the honours. No one disputed the right of the Bersaglieri to the second place ; Manara indeed claimed for them the first place, and declared that they also had lost 200 men that day.

. . . .

When once we have appreciated the true nature and extent of Garibaldi's failure in generalship on the third of June, which has often been exaggerated and as often unduly minimised, there is no propriety in offering excuses such as that he was ill, or that his talent was for the open field. In the eyes of Rome, and of the survivors among the regiments which he had led to the slaughter, he needed no excuse. Manara, usually very crisp in his criticisms of men and events, describes the battle in a private letter without breathing a word against Garibaldi, and instead of calling him " a devil and a panther," as he had done a month before when he did not know him, only says " the poor General lost his best officers." Every one knew that Garibaldi had commanded badly ; no one loved him the less, and no one was less eager to fight and die under his orders. His popularity during the month of siege that followed was greater than ever, and the reason is not far to seek. He had given his countrymen what the national instinct craved for at that moment more than for victory—honour. It was not tactics but heroism for which Italy was athirst in that year of despair crowned and glorified by faith. If, a decade later, he had lost battles in Sicily, if he had failed to maintain his hold on the terraces of Calatafimi, if he had been driven back out of the streets of Palermo, it would have been irretrievable disaster and uncompensated loss. But, in 1849, the present was but the seedling of the future. The heroism which he had inspired in the defenders of the Republic, culminating on this day of sacrifice, made Rome splendid as the capital of the Italy to be, and rendered the Temporal rule of the Pope henceforth impossible as an integral part of Italian life—possible only as a state of interregnum maintained by foreign bayonets.

For in times when new nations and new principles of government are being formed, men are
moved by appeals to the imagination—a fact too
often forgotten in our modern analysis of the
history of such periods. Imagination is the force
that propels, though state-craft may guide. In
such times statesmen, if they are as shrewd as
Cavour, build their subtlest diplomatic structures
on the firm base of an awakened national idealism,
feeding itself on great memories and aspirations.
But in order that men may aspire, it is necessary
that they should have something to remember.
And so the sacrifice made on the third of June,
and in the month that followed, of so many of
the best lives that Italy could give, had great
political, because it had great spiritual, significance. The noblest Italians had recognized the
eternal law of sacrifice, which Mazzini had first
taught them to apply to their own politics.
" Except a corn of wheat fall into the ground and
die—it abideth alone ; but if it die, it bringeth
forth much fruit."

Rome had to be won not merely from the grasp
of Oudinot, but from the force of the great traditions of Catholicism which had made it worth the
while of an opportunist like Louis Napoleon to
send these good French peasants and workmen,
dressed up in red trousers and blue coats, to shoot
and bayonet their Italian brothers. They had
been shipped across the seas for an idea. It was
the Catholic idea, the Catholic world, that had laid
its protecting hand on the Pope's throne. Against
the religious zeal which the Italians had defied,
they must oppose a moral force, or be beaten in

the end. In claiming Rome for themselves they had outraged the Irish, the Spaniards, the Austrians, half France, and many of their own countrymen. Vast spiritual agencies were at work all over the world to keep Italy out of Rome. Peter and Paul, Augustine and Loyola were rising from their graves to withstand Mazzini—the pale, frail Genoese, whose face was scarred with the sorrows of his country ; and this shadowy host could call up armed men from the utmost ends of Europe to defend the Pope. It would never be overcome except by a more living tradition, another cycle of tales of chivalry, a new roll of martyrs ; therefore the roll that had been opened in the Papal prisons was filled up on the Janiculum, and the best went gladly to the sacrifice. Some patriots, indeed, regretted that the defence of Rome was ever made, since it was so spendthrift of Italy's treasure : yet the treasure was profitably spent. Because men remembered and told with pride and anguish the story of the uncalculating devotion of those young lives in this hopeless struggle, there grew up, as the years went by, an inconquerable purpose in the whole nation to have their capital ; there rose that wild cry of the heart—*o Roma, o Morte !*—so magical even in years of discord and derision, that soon or late the Catholic world was bound to yield to it, as to a will stronger and more lasting even than its own.

There was needed, too, a warrior hero of a new type, rival to the figures of Charlemagne and the crusaders, who should win the heart by firing the imagination of Europe. And he, too, had begun clearly to emerge, and was likely ere long to over-shadow, more than was just, the fame of the Geno-ese who had begun it all. Garibaldi had now won Italy's devotion, and was helping to unite her divided children by their common pride in himself. Ere long he was to dazzle the imagina-tion of Europe—even of his enemies ; and to make his greatest conquest in the heart of the least impressionable but not the least poetical of races, the northern lords of the ocean.

But the chief glory of the third of June does not belong to Garibaldi, but to the slain—the seed that had fallen into the ground and died, and was to bring forth fruit in its season.

G. M. Trevelyan, *Garibaldi's Defence of the Roman Republic*, pp. 187–93.

On the day of their entrance into Naples and on the following day, Victor Emmanuel and Gari-baldi held private colloquies. The out-going Dictator asked to be continued in power for another year as the King's Lieutenant, and to have the grade of all his officers recognized. Such re-quests showed how utterly incapable Garibaldi was of understanding the difficulties of adminis-trative and military reorganization that confronted the new State.

On November 8 the throne-room in the Palace was the scene of an imposing ceremony, the official presentation of the result of the plebiscite, and the investiture of Victor Emmanuel with the Kingship of Sicily and Naples. The new monarch was seated on his throne. Garibaldi and his friends stood in one group, the courtiers and army officers in another, and small cordiality was shown between them. But the act of annexation was duly signed by all parties, and Garibaldi, formally resigning the Dictatorship, left the room a private citizen once more. His first act in that capacity was to publish a letter calling on all Italians to rally round Victor Emmanuel, and to be prepared to follow him next spring, a million strong, against Rome or Venice. " By the side of the *Re galantuomo*," he wrote, " every quarrel should disappear, every rancour be dissipated." Garibaldi's public utterances during this period of strained relations were as loyal as if every demand he made had been conceded by the King.

Before nightfall he sent Missori to tell the British Admiral that he would leave for Caprera early the next morning, November 9, and would come aboard the *Hannibal* to pay a farewell visit before he quitted the Bay. He spent the night in the Hotel d'Angleterre (or *Isole Britanniche*) in the Chiaja, talking with Missori, Mario, Canzio, Zasio, and others of his intimate friends. As during all these last days, he was in a melancholy and gentle mood, moving his followers to tears when he spoke of their parting on the morrow. In spite of the brave words of the proclamation in which he thanked his soldiers, and called on them to be ready against the next spring, all felt in their hearts the presentiment that their day of glory was at an end. And so these men, who had seized occasion by the forelock and had performed at the appointed moment the miracle never to be repeated, sat up all night in the hotel and talked sadly of what they had done and left undone.

Next morning, before dawn, they went down together to the port. The city was still asleep, and there was no one to witness the departure, which had been kept secret from every one except the British Admiral. They took a boat, rowed over to the *Hannibal*, and came up the side of the great three-decker, between the darkness and the first twilight. Admiral Mundy, still in his cot, was told that Garibaldi was in the cabin, and turned out with all haste to receive the strange man whom he had learnt to admire and love, while still keeping the open eye of common sense on his single-minded fanaticism. During a long talk in the cabin, Garibaldi invited Mundy to be his guest in his cottage at Caprera, " and spoke much of the beautiful harbour between the island and the main, where Nelson had once anchored for the protection of his fleet." As they passed up from the cabin to the quarter-deck, Garibaldi saw the Admiral's visiting-book lying on the small table upon which, six months before, at Palermo, he and the Bourbon Generals had signed the armistice, the source of such mighty consequences. He sat down and wrote in the book in French :

" G. Garibaldi owes to Admiral Mundy the most lively gratitude, which will last all his life, on account of sincere proofs of friendship with which he has been loaded in all kinds of circumstances."

As he went down the ship's side many of the officers and crew of the *Hannibal* were deeply moved, and the expressions which some of them afterwards used about "the look of intense love" upon his face testify to the unique effect of his presence upon men trained in no sentimental school of thought or character.

From the *Hannibal* he rowed to the *Washington*, the steamer that was to take him home. On her deck he parted from Canzio, Missori, Mario, and his other friends, who returned to the quay. His last words to them were "To meet again at Rome." Only his son Menotti and one or two persons of less importance sailed with him to the island. He returned thither as poor a man as he had left it in the spring. In the last two days Victor Emmanuel had offered him an estate for Menotti, the title of King's aide-de-camp for his younger son, a dowry for his daughter, a royal castle and a steamer for himself. But he had refused them all. His secretary, Basso, had borrowed a few hundred francs of paper-money from a friend, for necessary expenses. He himself had stowed on board the *Washington* a bag of seed-corn for his farm. With these spoils, the steamer, almost unobserved, left port at break of day.

He was soon back at his old daily occupations of man's primitive struggle with nature, at which, but for the call of a great epoch and a great cause, he would so readily have spent his whole life. Again the dawn and the twilight on the Straits of Bonifacio saw him at work among the granite boulders, industriously putting seed into the scrapings of earth which he called his fields; sheltering a few sad vines from the sweeping

winds of the Straits ; calling up his cows by name
from their pasturage among the wild, odorous
brushwood ; and seeking the strayed goats on
the precipice top.   Under these conditions the
melancholy of his last days on the mainland soon
left him.   When, a few weeks later, a visitor
came on business from Genoa, he found Garibaldi
" robust in health, and radiant with a calm and
serene joy."   For when once he had been left
alone again with his mother Earth, between rock
and sea and sky, no disappointment could prevent
him from feeling in his heart the truth that he
had done a mighty labour, and taken his share
in a task which the years would soon complete
and the long generations ratify—the Making of
Italy.

G. M. TREVELYAN, *Garibaldi and the Making of
Italy,* pp. 284–87.

Historical Material

AMONGST the Charlemont papers is an amusing
tale I do not remember having ever seen before
of young Philip Stanhope, the recipient of Lord
Chesterfield's famous letters :

When at Berne, where he passed some of his
boyhood in company with Harte and the excellent
Mr., now Lord, Eliott (Heathfield of Gibraltar), he
was one evening invited to a party where, together
with some ladies, there happened to be a considerable number of Bernese senators, a dignified set of
elderly gentlemen, aristocratically proud, and per-

fect strangers to fun. These most portent, grave, and reverend signors were set down to whist, and were so studiously attentive to the game, that the unlucky brat found little difficulty in fastening to the backs of their chairs the flowing tails of their ample periwigs and in cutting, unobserved by them, the tyes of their breeches. This done, he left the room, and presently re-entered, crying out, " Fire ! Fire ! " The affrighted burgomasters suddenly bounced up, and exhibited to the amazed spectators their senatorial heads and backs totally deprived of ornament or covering.

Young Stanhope was no ordinary child. There is a completeness about this jest which proclaims it a masterpiece. One or other of its points might have occurred to any one, but to accomplish both at once was to show real distinction.

Sir William Stanhope, Lord Chesterfield's brother, felt no surprise at his nephew's failure to acquire the graces. " What," said he, " could Chesterfield expect ? His mother was Dutch, he was educated at Leipsic, and his tutor was a pedant from Oxford."

Papers which contain anecdotes of this kind carry with them their own recommendation. We hear on all sides complaints—and I hold them to be just complaints—of the abominable high prices of English books. Thirty shillings, thirty-six shillings, are common prices. The thing is too barefaced. His Majesty's Stationery Office set an excellent example. They sell an octavo volume of 460 closely but well-printed pages, provided with an excellent index, for one shilling and elevenpence. There is not much editing, but the quality of it is good.*

If any one is confined to his room, even as Johnson was when Malone found him roasting apples and reading a history of Birmingham, he cannot do better than surround himself with the publications of the Historical Manuscripts Commission ; they will cost him next to nothing, tell him something new on every page, revive a host of old memories and scores of half-forgotten names, and perhaps tempt him to become a confirmed reader.

AUGUSTINE BIRRELL, *Collected Essays* (1922),
III., 219 (first printed 1906).

The Use of Historical Materials

IT was a propitious moment for all the friends of disorder. In Flanders the little army of Charles II. was waiting for a chance to cross the water ; in England the Royalists were preparing for an immediate rising, and the Marquis of Ormond, hidden in London, was inspecting the preparations and arranging for concerted action between the different sections of his party. All this the Protector knew, and his government was preparing to meet the danger. On February 3 the House of Lords, on behalf of the government, sent two of the judges as messengers to the Commons asking them to join in an address to the Protector for banishing all Papists and Cavaliers twenty miles

* His Majesty's Stationery Office still publishes such historical material ; but, alas, no longer at this price !—ED.

from London. The Commons, wrapped up in disputing about the title, simply replied that they would send an answer " to the other House " by messengers of their own, and continued to wrangle. Against the Fifth-Monarchy men and the Anabaptists Cromwell had already taken his precautions. On February 3 he signed a warrant to the Lieutenant of the Tower for the arrest of their leaders, Hugh Courtney, John Rogers, and John Portman, suspected of raising seditions and commotions in London. Their special offence was circulating pamphlets amongst the soldiers, containing adjurations to " destroy the Beast with his supporters." Signs were not wanting that the propaganda had met with some success, and that the project for the revival of the Republic had friends amongst the rank and file as well as amongst the officers. Soldiers had been heard to speak of the sinfulness of " enthralling their posterity, though themselves might live well for a time," and it was known that the Protector's own regiment of horse was of doubtful fidelity. On the night of February 3 the Protector took the precaution of making the guards at Whitehall, Westminster, and the Mews change places with each other, so as to prevent any possible collusion between them and the disaffected party. More and more, as fresh information reached him, he became convinced that nothing but immediate action on his part could prevent a demonstration against the government so serious that the public peace might be endangered. Therefore, without consulting any of his Council, he resolved, on the morning of February 4, to prevent the presentation of the petition by dissolving Parliament. As secrecy was essential he did not even communicate his intentions to Secretary Thurloe, who was ill in bed, telling him simply that he was going to the House, but not saying why. About ten o'clock he left Whitehall by the back way, intending to take a boat to Westminster as he had done when he opened the session. But the ice in the river was so bad that it was impossible to go by water. He came back therefore, and told the first of his guards he met to press the nearest coach he could find. For the need of haste was so great that he could not wait for one of his state coaches to get ready. The guard did as he was ordered; and so in a hired hackney coach drawn by a couple of horses, attended only by four footmen and five or six guards, the Protector made his way to the House, which he reached between ten and eleven.

Arrived at the House Cromwell retired into " the withdrawing-room " he usually made use of on his visits, and refreshed himself by drinking a cup of ale and eating some toast. At the same time he sent to call the judges from their courts in Westminster Hall, and ordered Black Rod to summon the Commons to meet him in the Lords' House. Fiennes and Fleetwood, hearing of his presence, came to him in the withdrawing-room, anxious to learn the meaning of his unexpected arrival. Fiennes asked him what he intended, to which he said that he would dissolve the House. " I beseech your Highness," said Fleetwood, " consider well of it first; it is of great consequence." " You are a milksop," replied the

Protector to his son-in-law; "as the Lord liveth I will dissolve the House." Paying no further attention to their remonstrances, he proceeded into the Lords' House, and, standing under the cloth of state, addressed the now assembled members.

To the Commons this sudden summons to meet the Protector was a great surprise. They had met as usual at nine o'clock, and proceeded, as usual also, to debate " touching the appellation of the Other House." Baron Thorpe had made a long speech against calling them Lords without first limiting the powers they might claim by virtue of that title. Serjeant Maynard had argued with equal learning that " Lords " was the only possible name by which the " Other House " could be called, and that it was a salutary thing to have such a check on the Commons. As Maynard ended, the Speaker announced that Black Rod was at the door. Up jumped Scot to make his ninth or tenth speech on the same subject, and avail himself of what he suspected might be his last opportunity. An obscure member interrupted him, saying that he had spoken to the question already, and had promised to speak no more; while Haslerig intervened to suppress the obscure member and back up his friend Scot. Others reminded Haslerig that Black Rod was waiting. " What care I for the Black Rod ? " retorted Haslerig wrathfully. " The gentleman ought to be heard." The two would have disregarded the Protector's messenger, for they guessed what his appearance meant ; but the House gave them no support. Black Rod delivered his message :

" Mr. Speaker, his Highness is in the Lords' House and desires to speak with you." So the debate was adjourned and the members trooped after their Speaker to hear what his Highness had to say.

The last time he met them, began the Protector, he had " very comfortable expectations " that the meeting of this Parliament would be a blessing to these nations. He owed his present position of Protector to the Petition and Advice which the House of Commons had presented to him. Not a man living could say he sought it. When they petitioned and advised him to undertake this government, he had told them he thought the burden too heavy for any creature ; and he had refused to undertake it except upon certain conditions, to which they had agreed. He had undertaken it in the end with great reluctance. " I can say it in the presence of God, in comparison of whom all we that are here are like poor creeping ants upon the earth, that I would have been glad as to my own conscience and spirit to have been living under a woodside, to have kept a flock of sheep, rather than to have undertaken such a place as this was. But, undertaking it by the Petition and Advice of you, I did look that you that did offer it unto me should have made it good." One of the conditions upon which he had accepted it had been the establishment of a Second House. " I tell you of one thing that I made a condition. I would not undertake it without there might be some other body that might interpose between you and me, on the behalf of the commonwealth, to prevent a tumultuary and a popular spirit. You granted it, that I should name another House. And I named it with integrity, I did. I named it out of men that can meet you wheresoever you go, and shake hands with you and tell you that it is not titles, it is not lordship, it is not this nor that, that they value, but a Christian and an English interest. Men of your own rank and quality, and men that I approved my heart to God in choosing ; men that I hoped would not only be a balance to a Commons House of Parliament but to themselves, having honest hearts, loving the same things that you love, whilst you love England and whilst you have religion. . . . I say I did choose such a House as I thought I might answer for upon my life, that they would be true to those ends and those things that were the ground and state of our war with the Cavalier Party all along. And what will satisfy if this will not ? "

In the second place, he would not have accepted the government unless there had been " a just reciprocation between the government and the governed " ; that is, unless those that represented the whole body of the nation would take an oath to make good what Parliament petitioned and advised him to do, just as he himself took an oath to observe the conditions of the Petition and Advice. When that was once agreed, they were upon a foundation—they had a basis to stand upon. As to any emendations or improvements they might afterwards think necessary, he considered himself bound to accept the advice of the two Houses. Therefore, if there had been " an intention of settlement," they would have ac-

cepted the constitution as a basis to be altered
or modified. But they had done nothing of the
kind ; they had sought to overthrow the existing
constitution and set up something else in its
stead. " It is evident to all the world that a new
business had been seeking in the room of this
actual settlement." Turning pointedly to the
members of the Lower House he added : " In
this I do not speak to those gentlemen, or Lords,
or whatever you will call them, but I say it to
you.

" You have not only disquieted yourselves, but
the whole nation is disquieted, which is in likeli-
hood of running into more confusion, in these
fifteen or sixteen days that you have sat, than it
hath been from the rising of the last session to this
day. Through the intention of devising a commonwealth again, that some tribunes of the people
might be the men that might rule all. . . . This
is the business ; but is this all ? . . . We have
known attempts have been made in the army to
seduce them ; and almost the greatest confidence
hath been in the army to break and divide us. . . .
I have seen the tendency of these things to be
nothing else but the playing of the King of Scots
his game, by beginning tumults and disturbances
amongst us. . . . What I told you at the last
meeting in the Banqueting House is more confirmed to me within a day or two than I knew
then : that the King of Scots hath an army drawn
down towards the waterside ready to be shipped
for England. I tell you that I knew this from their
own mouths and from eye-witnesses of it, that
they are in a very great preparation to attempt

upon us. And whilst that is doing, there are endeavours from some not far from this place to stir up the people of this town into tumulting. . . . It is not only that, but endeavours hath been to pervert the army whilst you have been sitting, and to draw them to state the question about a commonwealth."

If these things were so, what could it all end in but blood and confusion ? And what was the cause but their not assenting to what, by the Petition and Advice, they had forced him to accept ?

" If this be the end of your sitting and this your carriage I think it high time that an end be put to you sitting. And I do declare to you here that I do dissolve this parliament. And let God be judge between you and me." " Amen," answered some of the Commons.

C. H. Firth, *The Last Years of the Protectorate, 1656–1658*, II., 34–41.

In Search of a Fact

From the castle we turned into the town—if so shrunken a place could merit such a name. The *posada* did not invite to coffee, so we passed on up the small street, hung, as is usual in Spain even in the remotest villages, with electric light, just a single wire and a bulb of two or three candle power. In a small plot beside the church children were playing, despite the full blaze of the westering sun ; and the brightest of them answered an enquiry for the keys by running off to fetch the sextoness. After a struggle with the lock she let us into a big barnlike structure, whitewashed beyond hope, and striking sharply cold after the heat outside. Here at length were the Tombs of the Fonsecas, four white marble effigies recumbent on long slabs which gave ample room for inscriptions—one in either transept, one north and one south of the altar.

.   .   .   .

But it was the second who interested us most, Fernando's brother, an earlier Alonso who had been Archbishop of Seville (†May 18, 1473), and *primer fundador de esta casa.* Here was the reward of our trudge under the sun, the reward of our thirst. This Alonso had been the patron of Antonius Nebrissensis, that famous Spanish scholar who with Ximenes' support had placed Spain in the van of the contest for the Revival of Learning. Now the chronology of Antonius' life is unsettled, and depends on various statements which he makes incidentally in his works. He was born in 1444, the year before the civil strife at Olmedo, was so many years at Salamanca, went at nineteen to Bologna, then so many years with Fonseca, so many again at Salamanca, so many with Stunica (†1504), a later Archbishop of Seville; and when the figures are added together, they amount to too many, more than the sixty allowed by the limits given. For a midway point the date of Fonseca's death was wanted; and for this recognized authorities could give nothing more sure than 1473, with a query—not a date to reckon from, though a late manuscript in Madrid added May 18. But here on his tomb was an authority beyond which one need not seek, the date of his death graven securely on stone.

P. S. ALLEN, " A Castle in Spain," reprinted in *Erasmus, Lectures and Wayfaring Sketches,* pp. 186–88 (first printed 1914).

Economic History in Rags

THERE was some evidence, in the years 1901–14, of a slight deterioration in standards of living—not, of course, as compared with 1815, 1845, or 1875, but as compared with the favoured nineties. " Natural " causes connected with price movements were not entirely responsible. The policies of the armed peace and economic self-sufficiency had to be paid for both in France and Germany. German economists admitted that, with an equal expenditure, an English workman was better fed than a German. And English specialists noted, in the ten years before the war, that German rags were not quite so good as they used to be. This is a sure test ; for prosperous nations and classes throw away their clothes early. The best rags on the market are American and Canadian ; the worst Italian and Greek.

J. H. CLAPHAM, *Economic Development of France and Germany, 1815–1914,* pp. 406–7 (1921).

Evidence

I THINK one feels in German work the absence of that habit of weighing evidence and attributing to it its full weight, nothing more and nothing less, which generations of jury practice have made a second nature to the English intellect.

L. CREIGHTON, *Life and Letters of Thomas Hodgkin,*
p. 415.

What is Truth ?

THE battle [of Agincourt] will always be remembered for the enormous slaughter of the vanquished, especially among their high-born leaders. The French had lost the bulk of their nobility and amongst their dead were numbered the Dukes of Alençon, Brabant, and Bar (with his brother John), the Constable of France, Charles d'Albret (to whose weakness and mismanagement the chief blame for the disaster must always attach), the Admiral Jacques de Châtillon, Lord of Dampierre, together with Philip, Count of Nevers, another brother of the Duke of Burgundy, Terry, Count of Vandemont, Robert, Count of Marle, the Counts of Blamont, Grandpré, Roncy, Dammarton, Fanquembergues and Vancourt, together with ninety lords, over 1,560 knights, and between 4,000 and 5,000 men-of-arms. These were all " worthy men " or " gentlemen in coat armour," and some record of them was said to have been made by the heralds, while the nameless herd was never even counted up. In England the gross total of the French killed was set down roughly at from 10,000 to 15,000, though the belief was certainly current with the man in the street that 11,000 would cover the total loss both of killed and prisoners, and with this calculation the soberest French estimate is not seriously at variance, though in the first shock of their distress their writers likened their losses to the ears of corn in Beauce or the grains of sand in the Loire, so great that no man could number them.

On the English side the casualties were wholly insignificant. Elmham indeed will own to the loss of no more than 13 or 15 "persons," though some will go as high as 16, 20, 25, 26, 27, 28, 30, 33 or even 40, and though we may try to make sense of this by interpreting persons as "personages" or "men of name," yet it is certain that the writers who used the word meant to include all ranks, while the apparently official report still preserved at Salisbury which gives the number of the English dead at "about 15" expressly calls them "varlets," adding "of lords no more than the Duke of York and the young Earl of Suffolk." Much ridicule has been cast upon these curious figures by later writers who rejected them as "beyond belief," because they are so "inconceivably small," and they certainly seem to reach their climax of absurdity in Elizabethan times when the public were told that the English losses were "not above 5 or 6 and no common soldiers," or in the ballad where "thousands of Frenchmen fall to *one*." But the figures undoubtedly found acceptance with well-informed contemporaries on both sides and were so absolutely accepted in England that in a Conversation Manual of the period written to teach French to Englishmen, where two travellers meet on the road near Rochester and talk over the latest news from France, the recent battle supplies the theme and the English loss is given as " 16 persons " besides the Duke of York and the Earl of Suffolk. In criticizing these figures it is to be remembered that there are other instances of heavy engagements with enormous losses on the one side and almost none on the other, while previous experience has shown that English archers when they had heavily-armoured men at their mercy could dispose of them in crowds with absolute impunity, and even the French believed that the English army suffered almost no loss at all but returned to England " whole and entire." Such statistics as I have found show four archers killed in the retinue of James Harrington, one man-of-arms (Henry Strete) in the retinue of the Earl of Huntingdon, while several names are struck out from the retinue of the Duke of York with the side-note "some captured, some dead," though even here the word dead (*mortui*) is distinct from killed (*occisi, interfecti*) and does not prove that they were killed in the battle. Thus though the English losses were as nothing when compared with the numbers of the French dead, there is no reason to doubt the French statement that they lost heavily in the first onset, while the mixing of the dead made it quite impossible to ascertain the exact number with any certainty. In Germany the number of English killed was believed to be 80, while with such French and English contemporaries as have committed themselves to details the numbers range from 100 to 600, with the notable exception of Monstrelet, who gives the total of all ranks at 1,600, and modern writers having a large field of choice have fully exercised their privilege of picking where they like. It is of some interest to note that 25 of the King's horses were lost in the battle, of which 6 were palfreys and 19 trotters.

. . . .

The usual plan has been to call out everything that is picturesque in the accounts of the various writers who narrated the events any time within the succeeding century and blend them together into a patchwork whole, provided that they do not carry contradiction on the face of them. My own effort has been to depend for essentials only upon the statements of those who saw the battle with their own eyes or had good means of information at the time, and we have seen that at least on the question of numbers most of these were obviously unfit to tell us anything that will bear examination. Foremost among the former group is the chaplain, Thomas Elmham, who was on the field from the beginning to the end of the fight and wrote down his account within two years of the events. Except in regard to his estimate of numbers his statements are quite exceptionally worthy of trust. John Hardyng was there in the service of Sir Robert Umfraville, but a long time elapsed before he wrote his Chronicle, and from the strangeness of his account his impressions must by that time have become much obscured. The same may be said of Jean Le Fèvre and Jean Waurin who were both present in the battle, one on the English and the other on the French side. But they were almost boys at the time, and when they wrote long after they had Monstrelet's chronicle before them and had compared notes with each other, Le Fèvre's memory being apparently the original basis of such personal recollections as they specially contain. Gilbert de Lannoy and his brother Hugh also took part in the fight, and both of them talked over their adventure with Le Fèvre, but in his own account Gilbert has little to tell beyond the fact of his own escape from being burnt alive. Of first-rate importance, though based on second-hand information, on the English side is the account of Thomas Walsingham which was written about three years after the event. Though it has an eye for stage effect and is embellished with quotations from Virgil and Persius, in its facts it is closely connected with Elmham's account, and the same may be said of the ballad on the siege of Harfleur written about twelve years later still, and the narrative of the Italian Tito Livio who was in intimate communication with the Duke of Gloucester who was wounded in the battle. On the French side Pierre de Fenier was a native of the county of Artois and was connected with Beauquesne and Doullens all on the line of march, and when he died in 1433 he was buried in the church of St. Nicaise at Arras. Thus all his personal interests were in the neighbourhood of the battle but his account of it has little local colour. Guillaume Gruel in writing the life of his master, Arthur, Count of Richmond, had his material from the lips of the Count himself who was wounded and captured in the fight. The Count was thirty-seven years of age when he gave his biographer the information,

but by that time the battle was so remote an event
that he did not seem to realize the need for
accuracy ; while Alain Chartier wrote his poem
of the " Ladies " very soon after the disaster, but
it deals rather with the sequel of the fight than
the details of the fight itself. The Diary of the
so-called Bourgeois reflects the bitterness of anti-
Armagnac feeling in Paris, and the poem of the
Pastoralet is likewise a Burgundian lament. The
Monk of St. Denys gleaned the fullest information from the neighbourhood of the court, but his
sober narrative is taken up and spoiled with a
strong Orleanist bias by the Armagnac, Jean
Juvenal des Ursins, who wrote under the sting of
exile at Poitiers some fifteen years after the event.
If the Monk of St. Denys makes the Frenchmen
ankle-deep in mud, he puts them in up to calf
of the leg ; if the monk says straight out that the
French horsemen turned tail and fled, Juvenal
says that their horses swerved and so some people
fancied they were running away ; and if the
monk avers that the English arrows pierced the
Frenchmen's basnets he says that they did no
harm because the French were well protected, but
that they broke down at close quarters because
they were out of breath. He lays imaginary
ambuscades in the woods. He multiplies the
number of prisoners by ten, and when eye-
witnesses declare that the Frenchmen lowered
their heads to escape the English volleys, he says
they did it to avoid the blinding sun, forgetting
apparently about the pelting rain that plays so
essential a part in all the earliest accounts. Much
valuable first-hand information is contained in an

account known as the Chronicle of Ruisseauville, which was certainly written after the death of Henry V. and is remarkable for the writer's animosity towards the Constable d'Albret, Gaucourt, and Clignet de Brebant, all three of whom he regards as traitors, while he has nothing to say against the English, but goes out of his way to blacken the French (*i.e.* the Armagnacs) for robbing the poor fugitives from Harfleur, and robbing towns, churches, and monasteries.

.   .   .   .

But if some such warning is essential in probing the moral lessons of the battle, far more essential is it when we try to deal with details from the point of view of strategy. For it did not take long before swarms of circumstantial myths began to gather round the story, and so deeply have they struck their roots that we may almost despair of ever again being able to read it in its original simplicity. The archers, for example, in the earliest accounts merely carry each man his stake instead of a pavise, prick them in the ground like a hedge in front of them, and rush forward after the French charge has been baffled, but in modern writers the stakes get "interlaced" into a rampart, a palisade, whether fixed or portable, a breastwork, a barrier, an entrenchment, a stockade, an *enceinte* or *chevaux de frise* behind which the archers "nimbly retreat with a wonderful discipline." Some writers invent a body of pioneers or billmen to move this "fortification" about "as should be directed," plucking it up and pleaching it again and again. Some make the archers fix their stakes in front of them, some at the side, some even at the back ; others suppose that after fixing them up in front they left them behind them sticking in the soil, while some think that the ground was so soft that the stakes would not stick in the soil at all. Some, as we have seen, station the archers on the wings, some in the front, some put the men-of-arms between the archers, some the archers between the men-of-arms, and so on, with all possible permutations. One starts the difficult hypothesis that they threw their stakes " out of their hands so that one end should stick in the ground while the other stood out aslant, *with the point towards the enemy*," a boomerang-feat which would certainly seem to have demanded a good deal of previous rehearsal.

Again, an early writer speaks of the French army as " barring the passage " to Calais—*i.e.* as they stood posted in front of the woods of Azincourt and Tramecourt, and when the French vanguard was broken by the onrush of the maddened horses he quite naturally says that they were " in a great strait," but the harmless " strait " and the necessary " passage " have now become a " deep gorge " or " lane," a " narrow Valley," a " veritable defile," three miles long and anything from 700 feet to a mile and a half wide, in which the whole French army was " cooped up " and " imprisoned," undulating either between two woods, or two roads, or two rivers, a wood and a river, or a hedge and a bank, a hedge and a ditch, or a plateau and a slope, and " jammed in " so close together that they could not lift an arm. And this passion for woods has been spread across to the English position also, and some writers even not content with stationing each of the two armies between its own couple of woods place another wood in the intervening space between them, with this difference, however, that whereas the lateral woods are the ruin of the French, they become the means of salvation to the English, who " just fill the space " between hedges and brushwood, rills, coppices, orchards, thickets, briars, bushy meadows, " rising ground covered with trees and thick bushes," and " inaccessible woods " which act as " impregnable and invincible outposts," all of which arises seemingly from statements by Elmham that the flanks of both armies rested on the woods, and by Titus Livius, who probably had not actually seen the field, that it was enclosed with hedges and thickets.

Quite early, as we have seen, these woods became the receptacle for imaginary ambuscades, and soon 200 English steal along " unperceived " by the French who are watching them in the broad daylight about a quarter of a mile away, and find their way into the wood at Tramecourt or into two of the woods, some putting archers into both, some archers in one and cavalry in the other, and some in a meadow quite close to the French front, but always without being seen in the broad daylight. From this vantage they turn the French in flank after they have thrown away their bows, they strike a paralysing blow at 8,000 heavily armoured Frenchmen, while another small body of English slip round into the very heart of the French position at Azincourt, and cause

irreparable damage by setting fire to a grange in
their rear. The first of these early fictions (viz.,
that of the archers in ambush) was looked into by
Le Fèvre, who distinctly states that nothing of the
kind happened, but the story is still alive, and no
modern account seems to be considered complete
without it. It is to be wished that the same
writer had also pricked the other early story of
an abortive night attack on the unsuspecting
English, which is supposed to have been made by
the Count of Richmond with 2,000 French horsemen. For in all these whimsical make-believes
we miss the real spirit of the adventure which is
a downright old-world hand-to-hand thrutch at
quite close quarters, in which there is no place
for craft or stratagem, and it is surprising how
modern narrators have failed to see that all their
guesses contribute nothing to a rational compre-
hension of it, but only land us far into the region
of the grotesque.

Thus the English are so out of food that for
two or three days they have been living on the
nuts that they could gather at the roadside, yet
when King Henry sees the Frenchmen sitting
down to eat their breakfast on the spongy ground
he at once " orders a plentiful refreshment " for
his own men too. Or how can we make anything
of a picture of the Frenchmen sunk up to their
knees, and their horses up to the hocks in mud
still performing miracles of valour, while the
English archers dance round them in the very
same mud, and " completely roll them over," one
writer leaving these " embogged knights " stuck
fast in the mud for a little while " in this un-

enviable position," and then supposing that they
" broke and turned to the rear " ? In presence
of such large absurdities, it becomes a minor
matter to note that the space between the con-
tending armies is given at anything between 20
paces and 3 miles ; that some writers put the
English on " heights difficult of access," others
place both armies on slightly elevated ground,
others again have both armies in valleys with an
intervening hill, others give the hill to the French
and put the English in a valley, while others place
the French in a valley, though exact measurements
prove that the difference of level between Maison-
celles and the cross-roads is really less than 10
feet, so that the whole field is practically flat as a
table. One says that the " height " hid them
from each other's view and that they climbed up
it in silence, though we know that they shouted
loud war-cries as they advanced, while with
others the earth " shakes with their quick and
single tramp " in spite of the " mud clinging to
their thick soles." Some place the fight in front
of Azincourt, some to the rear, some on both
sides of it, some both in front and rear, and some
quite away from the village altogether. Some
arrange the English in three lines, some in two,
and some in one, with the same uncertainty about
the formation of the French. Some put the
French on horseback and the English on foot,
others think that the French were " mostly
mounted," or half of them mounted, while others
make all the lances fight on horseback, though it
is perfectly clear that with the exception of the
squadrons of cavalry on the French wings all the

fighting was done on foot. Some strip the archers naked, others " almost naked," others naked to the waist, others picture them naked below the waist, others as hatless and bare-legged, and others in all these ways together, so that they looked like carpenters or brigands and " struck terror by their savage appearance." In short, there is not a single detail of the battle that does not get transformed or turned completely upside down somehow or somewhere, except the fact that the French lost and the English won. With some it is the French, with others it is the English who light fires in their camp. If the English king ordered perfect silence in his camp, the statement is countered by another that makes his men blow trumpets and play all kinds of musical instruments in spite of their fatigue, and so the ominous stillness that alarmed the French becomes a trumpeting of horns and hautboys and pipes and fiddles that fills the air all night, and when this fiction has sufficiently taken root, speculation starts as to whether the order to play was given before the order for silence, or whether the English were enlivening their spirits with cheerful sounds to " raise their morale," or because they were brimming over with religious joy after confession, or to indicate their sadness and contrition, or only " imitating the familiar vociferations on the French." Again, notwithstanding the assertion that *both* armies are said to have been cleverly placed, it has long been the fashion to censure the French leaders for allowing themselves to be attacked in such a position, and especially to blame the " presumptuous incapacity " and " con-

summate ignorance " of the Constable D'Albret
as " a weak youth " without " talent or experience " or " the higher knowledge of war," and
that " few commanders could have committed a
more glaring series of blunders." But no sooner
have we lit upon the inevitable scapegoat, than
we are told that " there seems nothing to impeach
in the military distribution and direction of his
troops," that " the position that he had chosen
was perfect," and that " he does not appear to
have been deficient in the duties of a commander."
It seems a well-established fact that the night
before the battle was dark and that it poured with
rain, yet several modern writers give us clear
moonlight, while King Henry or " some competent officers " thoroughly survey the French
position, others apparently not believing in the
moonshine get the requisite light for him from
the camp-fires.

In presence of all these intricate contradictions
it becomes a matter of some importance to enter
a word of caution likewise against a peculiarly
subtle and fascinating form of self-deception that
will beset the student as he looks into the evidence
for the details of the battle. For in the general
dearth of anything approaching first-hand knowledge the Victorian publisher discovered that the
reader could best be allured to accept a theory if it
was illustrated by a plan or map. Hence arose a
great outburst of graphic representation in which
a succession of modern savants have tried their
hands at illustrating what they consider to have
been the tactics of the field, even recording the
changes at different hours of the day. But as

these sketches, when not directly copied, differ wholly from one another in setting out their pretty squares, oblongs, and triangles, with neat batteries of guns packed on either flank, they can but serve as a pictorial warning, and when we examine a few of them side by side they only help to emphasize the fact that we have not yet arrived at certainty in regard to the first essential details of that eventful day, and on the existing data I fear we never shall. But perhaps the most audacious explanation of the defeat is afforded in a recently published German dissertation. Starting with the belief that the defeat of the French is inexplicable on the assumption that they greatly out-numbered the English, and finding that all contemporary authorities both French and English are agreed that they did, the writer builds up a theory that all the known facts can be explained on the supposition that the French were really much inferior to us in numbers ; and when this theory does not fit in with such an episode as the offer even to give up Harfleur he courageously decides to throw over all the authorities on the ground that they were prejudiced Burgundians, and having nothing but his theory to guide him concludes that he cannot be far wrong if he puts the total numbers of the French at something between 4,000 and 7,000 men. After this all the rest becomes easy sailing and all previous descriptions of the positions of the armies whether by contemporaries or moderns are pronounced to be perverted and obscure. This curious theory of the numerical weakness of the French might well have been left to take its chance, but now that it has been adopted as the foundation of the most up-to-date account of the battle given by a very eminent writer on mediæval tactics it becomes necessary to emphasize the fact that it is based upon nothing but a purely fanciful hypothesis.

J. H. WYLIE, The Reign of Henry the Fifth,
II., 179–216.

Administrative History

THE object of the present work is to offer some contributions towards the almost unwritten story of English administration in the thirteenth and fourteenth centuries. The subject is a vast one, and materials for its study still survive in extraordinary abundance. Yet no aspect of our mediæval history has attracted less attention, and in no country has the importance of administrative history been so little recognized. There is no reason for entering with any detail into the causes of this neglect. Some of it is doubtless owing to our absorption in narrative history of the old-fashioned sort. Part is also due to the inaccessibility of printed material until quite recent times. A good deal of our incuriousness seems also to arise from our profound conviction that some aspects of our history are more important than others, and from our practical tendency to measure that importance by the light which past history throws on present conditions. We are still rightly proud of the English constitution, of the continuity between our modern democratic institutions and our parliamentary institutions of the Middle Ages, and of the way in which in modern times the English parliamentary system has suggested the form of free institutions to nearly every civilized nation. Accordingly, those interested in the history of institutions have thrown their main strength into the investigation of the parliamentary constitution and all that led up to it. We have our parliamentary constitution still, and it therefore seems practical and important to find out what we can about it. It is idle, it is argued, to examine institutions and offices whose vitality has long been extinct. We are no longer in danger of a despotism, and there is therefore little use in ascertaining how the despots of the past managed to govern the country. As a result, our natural absorption in the present has led us to study the past with minds too much set on present presuppositions. We seek in the Middle Ages what seems important to ourselves, not what was important to them. Given such a point of view, there is little wonder that few English scholars have troubled themselves to describe the minute workings of the machinery of the executive government during the later Middle Ages (pp. 1–2).

. . . .

As the whole ground of administrative history is still so imperfectly known, I was obliged to some extent to interest myself in the nature and functions of the chancery and the exchequer, and to devote considerable space to treating of these in print. However, so far as circumstances made it possible, I have striven to focus my work round those administrative branches of the royal household which, in practice, were constantly tending to become the rivals of the chancery and exchequer, and, therefore, a third great permanent element in the administration of the English state. Moreover, in studying the household on its administrative side, and the household administration in its public aspects, I have endeavoured, so far as possible, not to concern myself with the King's household as a whole. The daily life of the King and his court is entirely without my sphere. We shall have nothing to do with the pomp and glory of regality, and have little direct concern with the personal and domestic aspects of the royal establishment. Nearly the whole lay, and therefore most of the military, element in the household is foreign to my special purpose. Our attention must be fixed as far as possible on two chief aspects of household administrative activity. The first of these in order of time is the King's chamber, the source of the exchequer itself, which still continued to exist as a permanent domestic exchequer, even after it was overlapped, and to a considerable extent superseded, in this function by the King's wardrobe. But the wardrobe was never wholly or principally a board of finance. It was also, as Edward I. himself calls it, the " private chancery of the King." After dealing with the venerable organization of the royal chamber, I wish to describe the wardrobe as the chief administrative, directive, financial, secretarial, and sealing department of the household (pp. 18, 19).

. . . .

We have seen that the main reason why the wardrobe and chamber deserve some place in history is because they furnished the King with the best available instruments, both for governing his house and realm after his own fashion, and for withstanding the constant encroachments of the lay and clerical baronage upon his traditional prerogative. The effectiveness of these court organizations as administrative bodies was, however, largely due to their having the custody, and therefore the use, of special royal seals, called, in order to distinguish them from the great seal of the chancery, the King's small seals. In western Europe, where the notarial system had only a late and occasional vogue, no document was in the later Middle Ages in any sense authoritative without a seal. The chancery grew into the chief office of state because it was the place for sealing with the great seal. Because all sealing was done in France in the chancery, the chancery became the source of all the French ministries. The English chancery was less comprehensive in scope because of the liability of the great seal, in times of stress, to be withdrawn from the King's personal control, and because over against it a sort of domestic chancery was set up in the wardrobe. The wardrobe, not the chancery, was the place where sealing with the King's personal or privy seal was done. The history of the wardrobe, then, takes us to the history of the privy seal (pp. 22, 23).

.   .   .   .

A study of seals must more or less deal with what is somewhat grandiloquently called sigillography or sphragistic. Seals for their own sake may become, and often are, the subject of the merest antiquarian trifling. Yet there is no reason in the nature of things why seals, or their modern equivalent in the collector's view, postage stamps, should not in a humble way be made to contribute their little quota to the great work of reconstituting the past. To imagine the past correctly we must picture it in its minutest details ; because it is only by studying it in such a fashion that we can rightly obtain a sound conception of the structure and functions of bygone human society as a whole. But I have nothing of the seal collectors' special knowledge, and I have only a faint interest in the details of his quest. A seal is only important when it is studied in relation to the instrument it authenticates, when it is neither physically nor morally cut off from its natural place at the foot of its document and relegated to a show-case by itself (p. 26).

How dull and how unimportant are the details now set forth, no one can be more conscious than myself. But I have a profound faith, not only that the most trivial of historical details may be used to illustrate a principle of general importance, but also that the work most specially needed in English mediæval history is just the patient and plodding working out of apparently unimportant detail. By this method I believe the English mediævalist can best advance his science. If this supreme object can be attained, even in the smallest degree, it is irrelevant to say that the process by which it has been reached is technical and dreary (p. 29).

T. F. Tout, Chapters in the Administrative History
of Mediæval England, I. (1920).

Fiction and Fact

In speaking of the " fiction " of the peerage, no
allusion is intended to certain sumptuous and
annual publications, the genealogical contents of
which might fairly entitle them to that description.
Nor is it meant to deny that a work of fiction may
be good as well as bad. Fictions, and especially
legal fictions, have played a great and sometimes
a beneficent part in English constitutional history.
The presence of the King in every court and every
parliament in the empire is a useful fiction ; the
dogmas that " the King never dies " and can do
no wrong, are others of no less value. By means
of fictions judges have made law, and there is a
considerable element of truth in the claim that on
some occasions national legislation by the judges
over-rode the class legislation of parliaments. At
times the fictions of the courts have been strong
meat, and the identification of Cheapside with
" the high seas," which was once effected in a
court of law to bring a case within its jurisdiction,
marks perhaps the limit to which the process
should be carried. But the house of lords is the
highest court of law for civil jurisdiction in the
British Isles, and it is natural that there legal
fictions should have winged their highest flight.
Certainly no legal fiction runs counter to more
historical fact than the rule of the house of lords
that a special writ of summons to the Model
Parliament of 1295 entitled its recipient and his
successors to an hereditary peerage, and conse-
quently to a special writ of summons to every

succeeding parliament until his lineage was extinct ; and that if a commoner can to-day prove himself to be the eldest male descendant in the eldest male line of any one who has since 1295 been specially summoned to and taken his seat in a parliament, he becomes thereby entitled to a peerage of the United Kingdom and his blood is ennobled for ever.

Before we proceed to examine this tissue of legal fiction and its bearing upon the history of parliament, it may be well to enter a plea on behalf of the committee of privileges which advises the house of lords on peerage cases. Every one of the distinguished lawyers who constitute that court is perfectly aware by this time that this rule is based on a mass of historical falsehood ; he will none the less be bound in conscience to enforce it as the law. For the law takes little cognizance of historical fact until the fact has been interpreted by the law ; and then the interpretation becomes both fact and law. Once the interpretation has been accepted, the historical fact or fiction upon which it was originally based becomes irrelevant ; and no amount of historical investigation can affect the law. It is the law of the land that any one who proves himself the heir of a magnate of 1295 is entitled to a peerage. Not even the crown can debar him from it ; and the court is bound to enforce that law. It is also apparently bound to do far greater violence to historical truth, to interpret historic facts of the fourteenth century in the light of a law that was not evolved till the seventeenth, and to assume that when Edward I. or Edward II. summoned a man

by special writ to a parliament he intended to
create an hereditary peerage. From the point of
view of the court it is entirely irrelevant to prove
that Edward I. would not have known what the
phrase " hereditary peerage " meant, that he
never created or intended to create one in his life,
that scores of barons summoned by special writ
to one parliament were not summoned again, and
that no one for more than a century after Edward
I.'s death dreamt of claiming a right to a peerage
at all.

All this would be merely historical fact ; to
impress the court one must show that this historical fact had been interpreted as law. It is
fortunate for the peerage that the house of lords
can take no cognizance of historical fact which
conflicts with its own judicial interpretations. If
the house of lords says a commoner is a peer, he
is a peer, however inadequate or erroneous its
reasons may have been. A peerage adjudged to
a claimant on the strength of a forged pedigree is
not forfeited by the subsequent proof of the forgery.
A peerage adjudged to the heir general on the
strength of the presumption that it was created
by writ of summons is not forfeited by the subsequent discovery of letters patent limiting its
descent to the heirs male ; for no writs of error lie
against the house of lords, interpretation super-
sedes the fact, and the law is superior to history.
This, indeed, is common sense ; *quod non fieri
debuit, factum valet*. Much of the law of England
might disappear altogether if its legality depended
upon the historical accuracy of the claims to
peerage possessed by those who voted for it ; and

the legal foundations of the English church itself
would no longer be secure if the validity of Elizabeth's act of uniformity could be shaken by attack-
ing the pedigrees of three of the peers who
constituted the majority in its favour.

We are not, however, here concerned with the
legal validity of the lords' decisions, except to
point out that the law of the peerage is not
historical evidence, and that judicial theories are
as irrelevant to historical investigation as historical
fact is to legal decisions. The lawyer is bound by
judicial decisions which are more important than
evidence ; the historian is free. A judge can
make law in a sense in which the historian cannot
make history. It might indeed be contended that
historians have been responsible for not less fiction
than the courts of law ; but there is a difference.
The fiction of the courts becomes a binding law ;
the fiction of the historian only entertains the
student. It is only when history is merged in
theology that pontifical utterances are considered
decisive of historical problems. It is not the
historian's function to wear the black cap or to
speak *ex cathedra* ; his opinion constitutes neither
a sentence nor a dogma, and there are no penalties
for contempt of court.

The fictions of the courts and of the crown are
much more serious matters. *Solus princeps*, runs
a legal maxim, *fingit quod in rei veritate non est* :
supreme capacity for fiction is an attribute of
sovereign power. Sometimes it seems more like
the last resort of weakness, and some of the
fictions of the crown have proved an ever-present
help in time of trouble. Such were the rules that

an allegation of the crown could not be traversed, and that only those things were " records " which the crown could call to mind. The memory of the crown became the evidence for the fact. But it had in time to share its privileges with the peers and to acquiesce in the distribution of its sovereign power ; and peerage law is not a fiction of the crown, but the invention of the house of lords.

None of the lords' decisions have, however, summed up quite so briefly so much absurdity as the popular phrase " blue blood." It would hardly be worth while examining the fantastic implications of this expression of the theory of peerage, had it not been seriously defended by the latest historian of the house of lords, who writes with intimate knowledge of many aspects of peerage history. " The doctrine," says Mr. Pike, " is no absurdity at all, but one which is perfectly intelligible, perfectly consistent with itself at all points, and as scientific as anything to be found in medieval or modern literature." Neither medieval nor modern literature is perhaps the place to look for science, and it may be that this pronouncement is not intended to be so portentous as it appears. The obvious criticism, that the blood of the younger sons of a peer is just as blue as that of their eldest brother, and yet does not make them peers, is met by the explanation that the doctrine of blue blood, properly understood, does not mean that blueness of blood in itself made its fortunate possessor a peer, but makes him capable of inheriting a peerage. This may be comforting to a considerable number of Englishmen ; for there are some thousands of living descendants of our kings ; and there must be hundreds of thousands descended from the younger sons of peers. They are commoners none the less, and the blueness of their blood gives them no legal or political distinction whatsoever. If this is all that is meant by this perfectly scientific doctrine, it has nothing to do with peerage. For there is no mistake about a peer ; the legal and political distinctions between him and a commoner are clear and sharp enough, and they can be acquired without any pretence to blueness of blood. Moreover, in the middle ages the husband of a peeress in her own right, although himself a commoner, was often summoned by special writ to parliaments. Mr. Pike himself quotes the case of Ralph de Monthermer, who was summoned as Earl of Gloucester and Hereford in the right of his wife, but lost to her son the right to be summoned when that son came of age. He seems to have enjoyed that strange anomaly, a temporary lease of blueness of blood ! Into such vagaries can people be betrayed by mixing a physiological term like blood with law and politics. Titles to peerage have been decided, not by blueness of blood, but by royal writs and judicial decisions. If it pleases people to think that their blood was turned blue by a writ of summons or letters patent, and made red again by attainder, there is no harm in the superstition ; but it need not concern the student of the history of the peerage.

There are two serious problems to be considered. Firstly, what is " peerage," and how did it develop ? And secondly, how did it come to enjoy its present position in parliament ? The two are distinct questions, for there is no necessary connection between peers and parliaments, at any rate not in the modern sense of the peerage. But the word itself has passed through the whole gamut of meaning, from its etymological sense of " equal " to its modern implications of privilege. In the earliest Anglo-Norman legal terminology it simply denoted equality. Co-heiresses were said to be *pares* in respect of their father's inheritance, because all inherited equal shares ; a villein was described as the " peer " of other villeins holding of the same lord. There were, in fact, all sorts of peers ; we read of " peers of the county " and " peers of the borough " ; Valenciennes had twelve peers, so had Lille, and Rouen had a hundred in the time of King John. The *Modus Tenendi Parliamentum* implies that every member of a parliament was a peer, by dividing the whole assembly into *sex gradus parium*, clerical proctors, knights, and burgesses, as well as prelates and magnates.

But even before the Norman Conquest a limitation begins to be attached to the meaning of " peer " on the continent, a limitation arising out of its frequent association with the words *judicium* and *judicare*. Under Charles the Bald in 856 and Conrad the Salic in 1037 we find it stated that men are to be judged *per pares suos* or *secundum judiciun parium suorum* ; and in England from Henry I. to Magna Carta we have constant references to the principle *quisque judicandus est per pares suos et ejusdem provinciae*. Peer, baron, and judge come to be used as almost synonymous terms, though where a vassal speaks of his "peers" the king speaks of his "barons," because the king has no peer in his kingdom. By this time only those are peers who are equal to judgement, and this excludes the majority; *villani vero*, Glanvill tells us, *non sunt inter legum judices numerandi*. This is the meaning of "peers" at the time of Magna Carta. The idea that *judicium parium* in that famous document meant trial by jury has been too often exploded to need further comment. But it is material to our purpose to point out that judgement by one's equals meant that one was not to be judged by inferiors; it did not in the least mean that one was not to be judged by superiors. Our criminals are not the peers of our judges; and every lord of a manor could judge his villeins.

The "peers" are thus already a privileged class; they possess the right to be judged by their fellow-vassals in the King's court, and the right to judge their villeins in their own. They are also becoming hereditary, for these privileges are always attached to the tenure of land, and the tenure of land, though at first a mere life interest conditioned by service, grows more and more into irresponsible property. This process was accelerated by the creation of strict entails under Edward I. Estates now passed from father to son by right of heredity, and with the estates the privilege of exercising judgement, which seems to be the essential factor in peerage. By the end of Edward's reign England may fairly be said to have had an hereditary peerage.

But this peerage has as yet little to do with

parliament. There are many hundreds, possibly thousands, of these " pares," but Edward I. summons less than a hundred magnates by special writ to parliament. Those who sit in parliament have no hereditary claim to do so. The word " peer " does not occur in the " Rolls of Parliaments " for his reign, and it is not mentioned in his writs. It does not entitle any one to a special writ of summons, though probably every " peer " was either summoned in person or included among those from whom the sheriff required obedience to the general writs. But the " peers " still numbered their thousands, and included the lesser as well as the greater barons. It is clear, however, that the process of limitation, begun by the restriction of " peerage " to those who could " judge," was proceeding apace in the thirteenth century ; and the problem is to bridge the gulf between the number of " peers " entitled by Magna Carta to judge and be judged by their equals, and the smaller but still indefinite number of " peers " who develop into a parliamentary force under Edward II. The question is closely connected with the change in the *magnum concilium*. By what process were the thousands of tenants-in-chief, presumed to have gathered on Salisbury Plain in 1086, reduced to the " magnates " who gathered at Oxford in 1258 ? Or, in other words, how was the line drawn between the greater barons entitled by Magna Carta to a special writ and the lesser barons summoned in general through the sheriff ? For it is clear that the term *pares* tends to be restricted to the greater barons ; and the same question might be put in yet another form : what is the social and legal difference between one who holds a barony and one who simply holds by barony, or between one who holds *per baroniam* and one who holds *per servitium militare* ? The answer to any one of these questions should supply answers to all the others ; for the holder of a barony receives a special writ of summons, becomes a magnate, and then a modern peer. Even those who hold, not *baronias integras*, but *per baroniam*, are liable to the summons ; for, whatever " barony " may have been, it implied a special jurisdiction and a special obligation to the crown which conferred it.

Now it is obvious that the thousands who took the Sarum oath to William the Conqueror did not all hold baronies, and it may be doubted whether any definition of a barony had yet been evolved. But they were all the king's men, his barons, and they held their lands in chief by military service. The lands might be great or they might be small ; the extent would not affect the nature of the tenure, but it would affect the political value and importance of the tenant. Before long there is a distinction between barons and knights ; both held by the same military tenure-in-chief, but some are the king's barons, while others are only knights. Later there is a further distinction among the barons themselves ; some are greater and some are less, and the lesser barons are lost among the knights. By the time that the *Modus* is compiled, a rule has been elaborated by the king's exchequer to distinguish barons from knights ; the baron is the holder of a barony, and a barony is thirteen and one-third knights' fiefs.

Now a knight's fee is calculated at five hides, and if a barony was thirteen and a third times as much, it was two-thirds of a hundred hides. It is merely a guess that such an extent of land may have entitled a barony to be regarded as a private hundred possessing the jurisdiction usually connected with that unit of organization. But it does not appear entirely fanciful to conjecture that the individual holder of extensive lands was regarded as being entitled to special immunities, such as the right to exclude the sheriff from his barony, and exemption for himself and his tenants from attendance at the shire court, just as individual boroughs in later times achieved the status of counties. These and greater privileges had been granted to the earlier " honours," but from 1176, when Henry II. insisted that no " honour " should exclude the royal judges, there is said to have been little distinction between an " honour " and a barony ; and it is probable that these two kinds of " liberty " or " franchise " approximated. For baronies tended to be reduced in number and increased in size and dignity. Some fell into abeyance between co-heiresses ; others were accumulated in single hands by marriage and inheritance. The process which concentrated five earldoms in the hands of Thomas of Lancaster operated also in the case of baronies.

Now, while the grant of immunity from the shire court would not prevent the baron from attending if he chose, frequent complaints in the thirteenth century of the difficulties of holding shire courts owing to the number of "liberties" granted by the king indicate that voluntary attendance was rare ; and a rough division of labour and liability seems to have been in practice established. Lesser barons, who had to attend the shire court, were only summoned by a general writ to Westminster, the practical effect of which was probably a licence to stay away, and afterwards they were permitted to excuse themselves by sending a couple of representatives. But the greater barons, who escaped the duties of the shire court, were at least liable to a special writ of summons to parliament ; and it is probable that the divergence between knights and barons which had so powerful an effect upon the organization and growth of parliament had its root in an earlier separation in the shires. The barons held aloof from the local business of the people, while the knights busied themselves with its conduct ; and habits of co-operation and of management contracted in the shires were perpetuated in the national business of parliament.

Whatever its cause and method of operation, this discrimination between greater and lesser barons effected a change in the *magnum concilium*. If that name is properly applied to the concourse on Salisbury Plain, the adjective clearly applies to the numbers who attended, and not to their individual greatness. For baron at first means nothing but " man " ; and *baron et femme* is the regular Norman-French for " man and wife." But in process of time the *magnum concilium* became a small gathering of great men rather than a great gathering of small men. Greatness, not tenure-in-chief, constitutes the right or the liability to a special writ of summons to the

magnum concilium, which in the reigns of
Henry III. and Edward II. seems to have been a
council of magnates. It is significant that during
the interval of Edward I.'s strong rule, the adjective disappears from the council. His council
is a royal and not an oligarchic council; its
personnel depends upon royal writs and not upon
feudal privilege, and attendance is a matter of
obligation and not of right. But the idea of right
has grown up in resistance to the centralizing
policy of Henry II., the tyranny of John, and the
alien misgovernment of Henry III.; and it is
only for a time that Edward I. can check the
aristocratic claims of the greater barons to limit
the royal authority and participate in the control
of national affairs. The contest centres round the
council, its composition, and its powers. Is it to
be a council of magnates based on baronial rights,
or a council of royal advisers dependent upon the
crown? This is the issue between Edward II.
and Thomas of Lancaster, and it is during that
struggle that peerage makes its *début* as a constitutional force in parliament.

A. F. POLLARD, *The Evolution of Parliament,*
pp. 81–91.

A Study of Opinion

THE difference between the England of Shakespeare, still visited by the ghosts of the Middle
Ages, and the England which emerged in 1700
from the fierce polemics of the last two generations, was a difference of social and political

theory even more than of constitutional and political arrangements. Not only the facts, but the minds which appraised them, were profoundly modified. The essence of the change was the disappearance of the idea that social institutions and economic activities were related to common ends, which gave them their significance and which served as their criterion.

In the eighteenth century both the State and the Church had abdicated that part of their sphere which had consisted in the maintenance of a common body of social ethics ; what was left of it was the repression of a class, not the discipline of a nation. Opinion ceased to regard social institutions and economic activity as amenable, like personal conduct, to moral criteria, because it was no longer influenced by the spectacle of institutions which, arbitrary, capricious, and often corrupt in their practical operation, had been the outward symbol and expression of the subordination of life to purposes transcending private interests. That part of government which had been concerned with social administration, if it did not end, became at least obsolescent. For such democracy as had existed in the Middle Ages was dead, and the democracy of the Revolution was not yet born, so that government passed into the lethargic hand of classes who wielded the power of the State in the interests of an irresponsible aristocracy.

And the Church was even more remote from the daily life of mankind than the State. Philanthropy abounded ; but religion, once the greatest social force, had become a thing as private and individual as the estate of the squire or the working clothes of the labourer. There were special dispensations and occasional interventions, like the acts of a monarch who reprieved a criminal or signed an order for his execution. But what was familiar, and human, and lovable—what was Christian in Christianity had largely disappeared. God had been thrust into the frigid altitudes of infinite space. There was a limited monarchy in Heaven as well as upon earth. Providence was the spectator of the curious machine which it had constructed and set in motion, but the operation of which it was neither able nor willing to control. Like the occasional intervention of the Crown in the proceedings of Parliament, its wisdom was revealed in the infrequency of its interference.

The natural consequence of the abdication of authorities which had stood, however imperfectly, for a common purpose in social organization, was the gradual disappearance from social thought of the idea of purpose itself. Its place in the eighteenth century was taken by the idea of mechanism. The conception of men as united to each other, and of all mankind as united to God, by mutual obligations arising from their relation to a common end, ceased to be impressed upon men's minds, when Church and State withdrew from the centre of social life to its circumference. Vaguely conceived and imperfectly realized, it had been the keystone holding together the social fabric. What remained when the keystone of the arch was removed, was private rights and private interests, the materials of a society rather than a society itself. These rights and interests were the natural order which had been distorted by the ambitions

of kings and priests, and which emerged when the
artificial superstructure disappeared, because they
were the creation, not of man, but of Nature
herself. They had been regarded in the past as
relative to some public purpose, whether religion
or national welfare. Henceforward they were
thought to be absolute and indefeasible, and to
stand by their own virtue. They were the ultimate
political and social reality ; and since they were
the ultimate reality, they were not subordinate to
other aspects of society, but other aspects of
society were subordinate to them.

R. H. TAWNEY, *The Acquisitive Society*, pp. 12–14.

A Chapter of Misunderstandings

THE particular confusions with which this essay
is concerned are those between the council and
the privy council on the one hand, and between
the privy council and the star chamber on the
other. The first is so deeply ingrained in historical
parlance that professed historians commonly speak
and write as though the council and the privy
council were identical terms, and archivists themselves have not been exempt from the ambiguity.
Even Sir Harris Nicolas, to whom students of
constitutional history owe a deep debt of gratitude,
did much to propagate the confusion by inter-
polating the word " privy " in the title of his
collection of *Proceedings and Ordinances of the
Privy Council* ; and in the index to the first
volume of the *Calendar of State Papers*, *Domestic*,
all references to the council and its clerks are

summarily referred to the privy council. The
second confusion is partly due to the same lack
of discrimination. Even Leadam, who knew well
enough the distinction between council, privy
council, and star chamber, was once at least
betrayed into glossing "the starred chamber"
as "*i.e.*, the Privy Council." It also owes a
good deal of its vogue to antedating the truth in
S. R. Gardiner's statement that "the constitution of the star chamber had been admirably
adapted for the purposes for which it had been
used in the days of the Tudor sovereigns. Com-
posed of the two Chief Justices and the whole of
the Privy Council, it brought," etc. This was
approximately true for 1629, the year with which
Gardiner was dealing, but emphatically it is not
true that at any time in the sixteenth century the
personnel of the star chamber was limited to the
privy council and the two chief justices ; and the
antedating of the practical identity of the judicial
star chamber with the executive privy council
obscures one of the effective reasons why Stuart
government provoked so much more ill-feeling
than that of the Tudors.

The study of the council's history during the
Tudor period is, however, beset with difficulties
which may account for its failure to attract
attention. One of the first is a matter of spelling. It is impossible to deduce any conclusions
from the difference between "council" and
"counsel" in the sixteenth century as it is from
that between *consilium* and *concilium* in the
Middle Ages. Paget, the first clerk of the privy
council, spells his council almost uniformly

" counseill " ; his deputy, Sir John Mason, spells
it " counsell," with just an occasional recourse to
" councel." We have since differentiated " king's
council " from " king's counsel," but no such
specification was made in the sixteenth century ;
and it is between countless instances in which
" council " and " counsel " may be indifferently
used, that we have somehow or other to draw a
line to distinguish what was done by K.C.'s from
what was done by the King's council. For students
of the Tudor period the problem would not have
been more difficult had the English language, like
the French, derived one word instead of two from
the mediæval use of *consilium*. The truth of course
is that these modern categories did not then exist,
or at least had not been fixed ; and inasmuch as
they were not created but grew, we have to trace
beginnings which are almost imperceptible.

A more material, though not a less important
difficulty, arises from the original paucity or later
dispersion of the council's records. The council
was from the first an inner ring of the *curia*, and
inner rings are not addicted to public diplomacy.
Parliament and the courts of common law had their
rolls, but the council kept none. Some of its
records were filed, but many were not, and the
files were apt to disappear. Even when the council
sat publicly in the star chamber and came to
regard itself as the highest court in the realm, its
members occasionally argued that, inasmuch as
no writ of error could lie against it and its records
could not be called for, there was no need to keep
any records at all. The clerk, indeed, kept a
calendar of orders and decrees, but that was

apparently a private venture, and the volumes have not been seen since 1719. As for commissions, declared Richard Oseley, " an ancient clerk of the council in the court of White Hall," when examined on the point by Burghley, " I never heard or knew of any but from the Prince's mouth only." The student has often to deduce the position and functions of a particular official, not from any record of his appointment or statement of his duties, but from the salary he was paid.

A third obstacle in the path of the investigator is the unfamiliarity of the categories in which he has to seek his materials. We are always looking for sixteenth-century men and things in twentieth-century garb, and going for financial assistance to treasury and exchequer when what we want is hidden in the household and the chamber ; we can understand a lord high treasurer, who has nothing to do with finance, as little as a lord high admiral who never goes to sea, for the adequate reason that it was not his business. Neither in Hallam nor in Gneist will the student find the faintest allusion to the fact that the history of financial administration under the Tudors has still to be sought in the records of the household and the chamber rather than in those of the treasury and the exchequer. Similarly it is difficult to realize that the king's council was part of the king's household, just as a council was also part of the household of any magnate, and that we have to trace the development of the council with the help of household books and ordinances. It is from a household book that we learn that Sir Robert Cecil was once lord keeper of the privy seal.

A difficulty that has particular reference to the council and star chamber arises from the absence in Tudor times of our modern differentiation between a council and a court. Here again we read back into earlier ages a specialization of functions, if not a separation of powers, which did not then exist, thereby ignoring or confusing the process of historical evolution. Fleta's remark in the early fourteenth century is still true of the sixteenth : *rex habet curiam suam in consilio suo*. Council and court of star chamber, in the fifteenth if not in the sixteenth century, sit in the same room, consist of the same personnel, and exercise the same jurisdiction. The earliest known reference to the " court " of requests call it the " council " of requests ; the court of star chamber is the council in the star chamber ; and the other great prerogative courts are the councils of the north and of Wales and its marches. Courts are held *coram consilio*, and no one is ever summoned to appear before a *curia*. Even to-day the supreme " court " of appeal for the British Empire is the judicial committee of the privy council, which calls itself " the board." Much of the trouble that awaits the student is due to the fact that before the end of the sixteenth century historical writers and even clerks of the council themselves have begun to antedate a discrimination which by then was becoming clear, and to claim for each of the divided parts a history and traditions which belonged to the undivided whole. A clerk of the privy council, a clerk of the council in the star chamber, and even a clerk of the council in the white hall, will each contend that his particular

court or council is the King's council and the
true inheritor of its prerogative and prestige.
Archivists have perpetuated and developed the
confusion, and the history of the King's council
under Henry VII. and Henry VIII. has been
obscured because its scanty records have been
relegated to a category labelled the star chamber.
In order to trace the differentiation we have to go
back to the Lancastrian period before the differentiation began.

> A. F. POLLARD, " Council, Star Chamber, and Privy
> Council under the Tudors " in *English Historical
> Review* (July 1922), pp. 337–41.

The Second Empire

THERE was an agreeable spontaneity about the
Revolution of 1848 which it shares with the best
earthquakes. On the morning of February 22
Louis Philippe was King of the French ; before
sunset on February 24 France was a Republic.
The King's ministers were tolerably unpopular.
But then M. Guizot rather cultivated his un-
popularity ; and besides, it was one of the advantages of constitutional government that one's
ministers could be unpopular without imperilling
the dynasty. There was a faintly nauseous atmosphere of financial scandal. But revolutions
have always titillated rather than scandalized
French opinion, and it was hardly possible to
govern a nation with a lively imagination and a
peasant tradition of rapacity without giving cause
for some deviation from financial probity. The

edifice of the middle-class monarchy was not impressive ; but it had an air of bow-windowed security which seemed to promise an indefinite future. An incautious minister had just commented on the stillness of affairs ; it was the same calm which deluded Mr. Pitt into promising the House of Commons fifteen years of peace six months before his country went to twenty-three years of war, which led Mr. Hammond of the Foreign Office to observe to his Secretary of State that there was not a cloud in the sky as the black wrack of 1870 was driving up towards France.

But the world seemed very still in France by the grey light of February 1848. There was peace in Europe ; but its blessings are rarely appreciated until after an outbreak of war. French opinion was a little restless. The domestic felicity of an elderly king was becoming almost exasperating to a generation whose appetite for sensation had been pleasantly stimulated by the more adventurous morality of M. Eugene Sue and his less remembered colleagues of the *feuilleton*. A more disturbing taste for political heresies had been provoked by the almost simultaneous return of MM. Michelet, Louis Blanc, and Lamartine to the more spacious age of the Revolution of 1789 ; and it was improbable that imaginations which were playing round the great gestures of the Convention or the last drive of the Girondins would derive any lasting satisfaction from the parliamentary ingenuities of M. Guizot. The reigning dynasty was beginning to seem a trifle dull ; its attractions were ceasing to appeal to an increasingly indifferent public, and it was possible for Lamartine to summarize the shrug of a nation's shoulders in his bitter phrase " *la France s'ennuie.*" But revolutions are rarely the result of boredom, and France in February 1848 seemed very far from revolution. A number of preposterous persons had distilled from the tedious science of political economy a queer nostrum called Socialism, with which they mystified their patient proletarian audiences. But their doctrine seemed at once too good and far too logical to be true, and their strange incitements cast hardly a shadow on the political scene. The centre of the stage was held by a more blameless company. A number of rather solemn gentlemen who formed the constitutional opposition raised the respectable banner of Reform ; their impeccable programme included an extension of the franchise and the exclusion of public servants from politics, and they exploited with a rather childish glee the British institution of the political dinner. The *Banquets Reformistes* were a novelty in French political agitation ; provincial caterers were delighted with enormous orders, and long tables were spread in public gardens at which prominent politicians gave sonorous displays of their public virtues. There was a post-prandial alliance of Orleanist radicals and the more respectable republicans, and the deep notes of M. Odilon Parrot mingled with the shriller accents of MM. Garnier-Pages and Ledru-Rollin in condemnation of the existing government. It was regarded officially as a harmless exercise, until the reformers proposed to conclude the series with a monster demonstration in Paris. After a little fumbling the function was proclaimed by the Government. It was to have been held on February 22. On that morning Louis Philippe was still King of the French ; two days later France was a Republic.

The day of the great meeting (it was a Tuesday) opened in rain over Paris. Soon after nine a crowd began to form outside the Madeleine, and there was a little aimless singing under the grey sky. For lack of any better employment, they made a move across the Place de la Concorde and marched over the river to the Chamber of Deputies. The building was empty, and a few minutes later the Dragoons trotted out of the barracks on the Quai d'Orsay and cleared the approaches. The old King was watching through field-glasses from a window of the Tuileries. He turned from the window to his papers ; and as he scattered some sand to dry a signature, he said to Horace Vernet, " *Quand je voudrai, cela se dispersera comme ceci.*" It seemed so on that first morning of the Revolution. A few windows were broken, and there was a little hooting ; the crowd sat round the fountains in the Place de la Concorde to watch small boys throw stones at the mounted police, and the Deputies began to walk across to the Chamber. In the afternoon the streets were gleaming with rain, and there was infantry massed outside the Palais Bourbon. The Dragoons sat their horses in their long grey cloaks, and somewhere outside a cavalry band was playing trumpet marches in the rain. Inside the Chamber an interminable debate dragged on about the Bank of Bordeaux, and on the great square the police were charging the crowd. There was a barricade at a corner of the Rue de Rivoli, and a few shots were fired. That night there was a great blaze in the Champs-Élysées, where some one had made a bonfire of all the park chairs, and in the late hours of Tuesday, February 22, the troops marched back to barracks. Paris seemed quiet, and there was little to show that by Thursday the Orleans monarchy would be a memory.

PHILIP GUEDALLA, *The Second Empire*, pp. 117–19.

On Footnotes

IT is pleasant to consider the various forms of lying, because that study manifests the creative ingenuity of man and, at the same time, affords the diverting spectacle of the dupe. That kind of lying which, of the lesser sorts, has amused me most is the use of the footnote in modern history.

It began with no intention of lying at all. The first modest footnote was an occasional reinforcement of argument in the text. The writer could not break his narrative ; he had said something unusual ; he wanted his reader to accept it ; and so he said, in little, " If you doubt this, look up my authority so and so." That was the age of innocence. Then came the serpent, or rather a whole brood of them.

The first big man I can find introducing the first considerable serpent is Gibbon. He still uses the footnote legitimately as the occasional reinforcement of a highly challengeable statement, but he also brings in new features.

I do not know if he is original in this. I should doubt it, for he had not an original mind but was essentially a copier of the contemporary French writers and a pupil of Voltaire's. But, anyhow, Gibbon's is the first considerable work in which I find the beginnings of the earliest vices or corruptions of the footnote. The first of these is much the gravest, and I must confess no one has used it so well as Gibbon; he had genius here as in much else. It is the use of the footnote to take in the plain man, the ordinary reader. Gibbon abounds in this use.

His favourite way of doing this is to make a false statement in the text, and then to qualify it in the footnote in such words that the learned cannot quarrel with him, while the unlearned are thoroughly deceived. He tells you in the text that the thing was so certainly, when he very well knows that it was not, and that if there is a scrap of evidence for it, that evidence is bad. Then he puts in a footnote, a qualification of what he has just said in the text, so that the critic who really knows the subject has to admit that Gibbon knew it too. As though I should write " The Russians marched through England in 1914," and then put a footnote, " But see the later criticisms of this story in the accurate and fanatical Jones." At other times Gibbon bamboozles the ordinary reader by a reference which *looks* learned and *is* inane; so that your plain man says, " Well, I cannot look up all these old books, but this great man has evidently done so."

.   .   .   .

The next step of the footnote in iniquity was

when it became a mask. Who started this I know not, but I should imagine that the great German school which remodelled history in the nineteenth century was to blame. At any rate their successors the French are now infinitely worse. I have seen a book purporting to be a history in which of every page not more than a quarter was text, and the rest a dreary regiment of references. There is no doubt at all about the motives, mixed though they are. There is the desire of the fool to say, " Though I can't digest the evidence, yet I *know* it. Here it is." There is the desire of the timid man to throw up fortification. There is the desire of the pedant to show other pedants as well as the general reader (who, by the way, has almost given up reading such things, they have become so dull) that he also has been in Arcadia.

I notice that when anything is published without such footnotes, the professional critic—himself a footnoter of the deepest dye—accuses the author of romancing. If you put in details of the weather, of dress, and all the rest of it, minutely gathered from any amount of reading, but refuse to spoil a vivid narrative with the snobbery and charlatanism of these perpetual references, the opponent takes it for granted that you have not kept your notes and cannot answer him ; and indeed, as a rule, you have not kept your notes and you cannot answer him.

For the most part these enormous, foolish, ill-motived accretions are honest enough in their actual references, for the greater part of our modern historians who use them are so incapable

of judgment and so lacking in style, so averse
from what Rossetti called " fundamental brain-
work," that they have not the power to do more
than shovel all their notes on you in a lump and
call it history. But now and then this temptation
to humbug produces its natural result, and the
references are false.

.   .   .   .

Here you will say to me what is said to every
reformer : " What would you put in its place if
you killed the little footnote, all so delicate and
compact ? How could you replace it ? How can
we know that the historian is telling the truth
unless he gives us his references ? It is true that
it prevents history from being properly written
and makes it, to-day, unreadable. It is true that
it has become charlatan and therefore historically
almost useless. But you must have some guaran-
tee of original authority. How will you make sure
of it ? "

I should answer, let a man put his footnotes in
very small print indeed at the end of a volume,
and, if necessary, let him give specimens rather
than a complete list. For instance, let a man who
writes history as it should be written—with all the
physical details in evidence, the weather, the
dress, colours, everything—write on for the
pleasure of his reader and not for his critic. But
let him take sections here and there, and in an
appendix show the critic how it is being done.
Let him keep his notes and challenge criticism.
I think he will be secure. He will not be secure
from the anger of those who cannot write clearly,
let alone vividly, and who have never in their

lives been able to resurrect the past, but he will be secure from their destructive effect.

HILAIRE BELLOC, " On Footnotes," in *On* (1923),
pp. 30–37.

A Picture of Peasant Life

WE may now pass from the general to the particular, and try to obtain such glimpses of actual recorded village life as shall enable us, little by little, to construct a coherent picture.

Let us take an abbey estate, as rather favourable, on the whole, to the peasant's well-being. Monastic charity was heavily counter-balanced by monastic conservatism ; but the reader will probably conclude with me, if his patience will follow me to the end, that there was a slight balance of prosperity, on the whole, in favour of the peasant on Church lands ; such a balance, perhaps, as there is nowadays in favour of government service. We will take, then, a great and famous English abbey like Glastonbury, with its many manors of varied soil, but more fertile than the average.

The abbot of this house was in every sense a great lord ; and one of the latest of the long series, Richard Beere, drew up a terrier in 1516, which describes minutely four of his ten manor-houses and parks. He may, indeed, have had more than ten ; the abbot of Bury had thirteen. With this wealth at his disposal, and this baronial dignity, he could do much even in the royal courts ; for instance, Abbot Whethamstede of

St. Albans notes in his memoranda how he expended, within a few weeks, something like £300 modern upon two judges and a sheriff. These English abbeys were small compared with the greatest in France, Germany, and Italy : " The great monasteries of France," writes Guerard, " were real states." But Glastonbury is a good typical example ; thousands of modern visitors go thither yearly, and for the past we have fairly full records ; therefore it affords a good frame for our concrete picture of peasant life. It lies in a beautiful country ; and its beauty is of the sort that would have appealed to all men in those days with which we are concerned. A friend familiar with Welsh village life has often told me the enthusiasm with which farmers have spoken to him after their first journey over the border, to Shrewsbury or Oswestry Fair : " England is a beautiful land ; it is as flat as a penny ! " Let us therefore repair to those rich stretches between the Mendips and the sea, dear to the farmer as to the artist, as flat as a penny, with their pastures and ploughland and woodland, and all the details described in Abbot Beere's terrier—warrens and fish ponds and natural meres, and the eminent great oaks in which the herons build, and the browsing deer below. Let us put back the clock of time by six hundred years, and imagine ourselves (if this be not too presumptuous) guests for a while of the lord abbot of Glastonbury. We have come from so far, in time if not in space, that he will not inquire too closely into our possible servile origin, but will gladly tell us what he can in exchange for the strange and moving stories that we can bring him from our own days. We shall stand with him at the oriel of his private chamber in one of these manors—let us say, at Wrington ; we shall watch the peasants coming home in the autumn twilight, for all the world like the peasant of to-day, each with his tools on his shoulder, and with the heavy gait of a man who was in no hurry this morning, and has still less haste after the day's work, even though supper be waiting for him. We ask the great lord how these men live ; what dues do they owe to the abbey ? He cannot tell us off-hand, but he bids the steward fetch his terrier ; and here, thanks to the diligence of Thomas Hearne the Oxford antiquary, we may look over his shoulder and read the very words.

Be it noted that each customary tenant [of Wrington] as often as he shall have brewed one full brew, shall give to my lord abbot 4d. under the name of *tolcestre*. *Item*, each customary tenant shall give mast-money for his pigs [in the woods], as appeareth more fully in the Ancient Customal. *Item*, be it noted that the customary tenants are bound to grind their corn at my lord's mill, or to pay a yearly tribute in money, viz. each holder of a yardland 2s. 8d. [etc. down to the lowest cotter at 4d.]. Be it noted also that when any shall die, my lord shall take his heriot, to wit his best beast. And, if there be no beast, from the holder of a yardland or half a yardland he shall have one acre of corn ; and from any lesser tenant, if he have so much land in cultivation, the lord shall have half an acre of his best corn. And, even though the wife die before the man, he shall give no heriot ; but if she die in the holding after her husband's death, and shall have given it up to my lord or shall die in her widowhood, my lord shall have the heriot as aforesaid. And if there be no corn, then my lord shall have the best chattel found in the tenement on the day of death, etc., as appeareth in the

Ancient Customal. . . . Note, that whosoever shall be tenant of the customary mill, which is now held by Edmund Leneregge, is bound to provide mill-stones, so that the burden fall not upon my lord, as was found upon the copy of William Truebody, lately tenant of that house and mill.

These are quite typical customs of the later Middle Ages, but we see at once how they take for granted and omit a great deal that we might like to have explained. But let us leave this for the moment, and mount with William Truebody to the church tower, and compare the bird's-eye view from that height with the same view as seen to-day. From Wrington tower we shall see more woodland, as in other parts of England we might see more fen, than at present ; the other church towers which look across to us will be not grey but white and new ; the villages nestling under them will have somewhat fewer and smaller cottages than now, and more widely spaced, each within its little garden or toft. But by far the most striking difference will be the comparative absence of hedgerows and the curious network of long strips in the arable field. This is the web within which the mediæval peasant lives and moves and has his being ; we must not strictly call it a spider's web, since his own forefathers have had much to do with the spinning of it ; but it is a very complicated tissue, which we must take into account before we can understand his daily life.

It seems certain that the manorial system of the Middle Ages had grown out of an earlier system in which common rights played a far greater part.

At the time we are considering, private ownership was recognized, but the exercise of that ownership was restricted. "Mediæval tillage was co-operative in character, and all the principal operations of agriculture were carried out in common." By the usual arrangement the whole land of the manor was divided into three "fields," each of which was ploughed and sown for two years running, and left fallow for the third. There are frequent traces, however, of tillage on a "two-field" or, again, on a "four-field" system. The lord had his own land, his "demesne"; the peasants had each a small holding. A full peasant had a *virgate* or *yardland* and two oxen to plough it. The normal plough-team comprising eight oxen, four such tenants would be associated in the ploughing. By the ancient laws of Wales, the land thus ploughed was divided every year among the contributors to the tillage, in order of importance; but there is no trace of this yearly redistribution in our England of 1324; each peasant has his own permanently specified lands in each of the three fields—with the exception of free labourers or landless dependents, whose status does not seem to have been sufficiently investigated. Besides the arable land there was nearly always a stretch of wood and waste, in which the tenant had certain rights of taking wood to mend his house or plough, and of gathering dry sticks and fallen timber. The familiar phrase "by hook and by crook" testifies, we are sometimes told, to those cases where the man might take not only the rotten boughs within reach of his arm, but also such as he could pull down with

a hooked pole. Then there were the common
grazing-lands, on which each tenant had his pro-
portionate right of pasture ; lands which, though
sadly shrunken, still survive in many places as the
village " common " or " green." Last, there was
the " Lammas-land," so called because it was
enclosed for hay from Candlemas to Lammas—
February 2 to August 1. These hay meadows
were very valuable, usually much more so than
the same extent of arable ; and they were not
only fenced in but kept under supervision by the
hayward, who takes his name not from the hay
but from the hedges which it was his duty to
guard. There were hedges also round the gardens
and tofts—a toft was, normally, a three-acre patch
which the full yardlander had round his cottage
—otherwise, all the land was open, and the
holdings were in long acre strips, divided from
each other only by " balks," or ridges of un-
ploughed turf, with " headlands " running trans-
versely along the tops of the strips to facilitate
access.

The arable, then, was divided into three " fields,"
each under a regular rotation of tillage or fallow.
One year, the field would be ploughed in October
and sown with wheat or rye, reaped in August, and
left in stubble. Next year it would be ploughed
in March, and sown with barley ; reaped in
August as before. The third year it would lie
fallow ; it was ploughed up twice in June, and
rested until the fourth year, when it would again
be ploughed and sown in October. Under this
custom (whether in two or three or four fields)
the individual peasant had no choice of date or of

crop ; he must plough and reap with the rest, and sow the same seed as they. As already suggested, the ploughing and reaping were very often done on a co-operative system; but it is scarcely safe to infer this too absolutely from the fact that any other conceivable system must have entailed almost incredible confusion and waste. For these holdings were mixed together in a very startling fashion. The lord's demesne was a sort of home-farm, tilled by labour which the serfs were bound to provide, or by free labourers whom the bailiff paid out of moneys with which the serfs redeemed their services. Yet demesne land frequently occurs in strips intermingled with tenants' strips. To some extent this was advantageous for both ; the tenant, having to put in a day's ploughing for his lord, could work at this adjoining strip instead of taking his plough and team half-way across the manor to work. But what shall we say of the subdivisions and complications among the tenants themselves ? The question of what became of a serf's younger sons (or elder sons, in the districts where the younger was the legal heir) needs more investigation than it has received, though it is much simplified by the fact that, owing to wars, pestilences, etc., population remained fairly station-ary during several centuries of the Middle Ages. But there was evidently a good deal of partition among the peasant's children ; this has been worked out with wonderful patience and acumen by Mr. W. Hudson in the studies to which I have already referred. He has succeeded in ascer-taining, with mathematical exactness, the sub-divisions in 1292 of two tofts—*i.e.*, a block of six

acres—which had once been held by Ivor Blackman, and are now divided among ten different
tenants. Only one now bears the original name ;
he is William Blackman, and he holds only three
perches, doubtless just a garden round his cottage; he was by this time superannuated, and the
main arable had gone to the younger generation.
Clement Rediere, again, is in an exactly similar
position. A third, Thomas Elsey, has likewise
his cottage and three perches, while around him
are other Elseys, doubtless his children, and
some Longs, between whom and the Elseys Mr.
Hudson traces a connection by marriage. Of the
remaining seven tenants, four have from an acre
and a half to just short of an acre, and three about
a quarter of an acre each. And, although this of
Blackman's tofts is the only holding which the
documents have allowed Mr. Hudson to map out
with this absolute certainty, yet all are similarly
broken up. Between Domesday and 1292 the
Martham tenants had naturally increased slowly
in numbers : from 63 to 107. But subdivision
had gone on at an enormously greater rate of increase ; there were now 935 holdings, in more than
2000 separate strips. Each tenant, that is, had on
an average nearly twenty separate strips, and these
might be scattered about anywhere on the manor.
We possess no actual contemporary maps of a
manor until after the Reformation, when the process of consolidation of holdings had already been
powerfully at work ; yet even those Elizabethan
and Jacobean maps show a bewildering maze
of tenements. There was probably, therefore,
some simplification of tillage by co-operation, and

Mr. Hudson's conclusion will probably hold for the majority of cases.

Why did the tenants rest content with the bewildering fractions of roods and perches, and how did they distribute the produce fairly ? We are not speaking of allotments which each holder can occupy with his own chosen crop. The whole 6 acres here were sown with the same crop. The divisions of tenancy were not marked. There could be but one way of distribution. The total number of sheaves of (say) barley would be divided proportionately according to the size of each tenant's holding and the due number handed to him or her. The reason why so many junior members of a family had separate portions of a holding was no doubt due to the fact that they were all expected to look after themselves even though living together. The age of maturity was entered on very early. A boy had to join a tithing at 12, which involved police responsibility, and he " came of age " at 16.*

At the same time, I think we must not assume that this, which seems to us the only business-like way of dealing with the tangle, was necessarily the way followed regularly and completely by the mediæval husbandman. In fact, one passage in *Piers Plowman* seems to point clearly to a good deal of private and separate ploughing and reaping ; the dishonest peasant confesses : " If I went to the plough, I pinched so narrowly that a foot-land or a furrow fetch I would ; from my next neigh-

---

* *Hist. Teach. Misc.*, i., 165.

bour nymen [*take*] of his earth ; and if I reaped,
[I would] overreach, or gave them counsel that
reaped to seize to me with their sickles that which
I sowed never." This evidence, I think, has not
been noted ; nor have I ever seen direct evidence
quoted on either side from the Middle Ages. On
the other hand, we have very direct evidence from
modern times in districts where mediæval conditions of land-partition survived.

W. Thoma, on p. 91 of his monograph on the
monastary of Leubus (Leipzig, 1894), quotes a
terrible account of the working of the mediæval
field-system in 1806, just before it was abolished.
The peasants declared to the commissioners :

that, of some 1,200 patches into which the domain was
parcelled out, a very large number did not even measure
half an acre ; the smallest were from 20 square rods to 30 ;
they went sometimes lengthwise, sometimes across at every
conceivable angle ; no man could conveniently arrange his
patches for sowing, because they were often too small to
plough. Those who had ill-drained land, if the autumn
were wet, could not leave it unsown in winter and sow it
in spring with some quick-growing crop according to
circumstances, partly because, in spring, they could not
get at their unsown land by reason of the other strips
which had been sown in winter, and partly because even
in summer, when the winter-sown crops had been reaped,
they would lose the sown summer-crops for want of being
able to look after them. The plots were so inextricably
confused, (they said), that nobody, even among the
interested parties, could tell exactly who owned this or
that parcel of land ; so that one interested party had
often happened to dung a piece belonging to his neighbour,
while another had sown and reaped it. Some plots lay so
that it was impossible to come at them except by driving
lengthwise or crosswise over intermediate plots ; so that a
terrible amount of seed and corn was ruined, especially in
seed-time and at the harvest.

It is probable that this confusion had grown very much with time ; and Silesia was one of the backward provinces ; but it must be evident that many of these difficulties were inherent in the system. In Flanders, Holland, and northern Germany, where abbots and great nobles drained swamps and cleared forest on a large scale, giving out the new land in compact holdings to tenant farmers, agriculture progressed far more than under the old conservative system. On such new lands, the tiller started with a clean slate ; he sometimes worked almost altogether outside the meshes of the manorial system, and could choose his own times and his own crops. The consequence was that the systematic growth of turnips and the regular rotation of crops seem to have been known in Flanders two centuries, at least, before they can be traced in England. Under our open-field system, the whole stubble was thrown open after harvest to the whole cattle of the community for grazing ; this rendered all experiment or innovation practically impossible. Each peasant must do as his neighbours did, and thank God it was no worse.

This is only one instance of the mediæval rustic's resignation to fate—or, shall we say, to a somewhat slipshod and disorderly Providence ? We have seen that the customs differed in detail not only from manor to manor, but even from group to group within the same manor ; so that these variations, like the rudimentary character of even the most definite arrangements, left room for endless misunderstandings and bickerings between landlord and tenant, or peasant and peasant.

One great difficulty, it will be seen at a glance, came from the minute and irregular subdivision of holdings. Each of these carried with it a similar subdivision of dues; as we have already seen, peasants themselves divided theoretically into fractions between different lords, so the peasant's services and tributes became correspondingly fractional, even down to half a farthing and half an egg.

Again, the wages were often given partly in food or in kind; to the peasant who for his workday could claim three herrings and a loaf, the age and condition of the herrings must have been very important; or again, if his wage consisted of a measure of corn, this depended greatly on the quality of the grain and the personal equation of the measurer. Moreover, weights and measures differed sometimes to an almost incredible extent from district to district, or even within the bounds of the same manor. At Martham, a perch of the tenants' land measured only 18 feet; but a perch of the lord prior's land measured $18\frac{1}{2}$. As Delisle points out: "the same manor had sometimes its large and its small measure; in more than one parish we find men measuring oats by a measure different from that which they used for wheat and barley." In France, under the *Ancien Régime*, there were literally hundreds of variations in the legal measures; and, even in England, where our fourteenth century kings tried to enforce a royal standard for the most important measures, exception had to be made for these manorial variations, and the peasant was left still at the mercy of local custom. . . . The personal factor and the

" sporting chance " are welcomed among folk
unused to standardization except in its most
rudimentary forces ; and the same trend of
thought may be traced in the Middle Ages.
Vinogradoff prints a series of customs which
may fairly be quoted as typical, from Borle[y],
a manor belonging to Christ Church, Canterbury,
in Essex.

And let it be known that when he, the villein, with other
customers shall have done cutting the hay on the meadow
in Raneholm, they will receive by custom three quarters
of wheat for baking bread, and one ram of the price of
eighteen pence, and one pat of butter, and one piece of
cheese of the second sort from the lord's dairy, and salt,
and oatmeal for cooking a stew, and all the morning milk
from all the cows in the dairy, and for every day a load
of hay. He may also take as much grass as he is able to
lift on the point of his scythe. And when the mown grass
is carried away, he has a right to one cart. And he is
bound to carry sheaves, and for each service of this kind,
he will receive one sheaf called " mene-sheaf." And whenever he is sent to carry anything with his cart, he shall
have oats, as usual, so much, namely, as he can thrice take
with his hand.

These scythe-fulls, these hand-fulls, these
sheaves, must have left much room for dispute ;
and often the measures are far more primitive
and disputable than this. Certain tenants of the
abbot of Ramsey had to go and collect " one hose
of moderate size full of nuts well-cleaned of their
husks." The history of costume shows us that,
at this date (1150–1200), such hosen came some
way up the thighs, but were not yet sewn together
into a pair of breeches ; they resembled the modern
cyclist's " overalls " ; Le Roux de Lincy has

recorded an old proverb to the effect that " short hosen need long straps." Part of the reeve's fee on a Glastonbury manor was " a stall full of [or a truss of ?] hay as high as to a man's loins." At the Abbey of Vale Royal, in the thirteenth century, part of the tenant's rent was " a reasonable pig," or " half a customary pig." The monks of Bern were bound to render yearly to the monks of St. Trond " twenty legal salmon." Certain peasants on Ramsey manors, when they had done a day's mowing, might " carry home so much grass or straw as they can bind in a single bundle and lift upon their sickle [or scythe] hand, so that the handle touch not the ground. And, if perchance the handle break, then he shall lose his straw or grass and be at the lord abbot's mercy, and pay a fine, coming to best accord that he can with the abbot." At another time, he may fetch from the abbot's farmyard a bundle of as much straw as he can carry, " but, if the band break before he has passed through the yard door, he shall lose his straw and compound by a fine as best he may." A reeve may take, at the end of his year of office, " the bottom of a haystack, of such thickness as he can pierce with one stroke of his pitchfork." After certain work, the servant may bring his own pitcher and take it home full of ale, up to a gallon, " but if the pitcher be more than a gallon, he shall be at the lord abbot's mercy." At Longbridge, under the abbot of Glastonbury, where the serf had a right to take one sheaf when he had reaped a cartload and carried it to the abbot's yard, a still more complicated method was used to secure a certain standard size for this perquisite. " If any sheaf appear less than is right, it ought to be put in the mud, and the hayward should grasp his own hair above his ear, and the sheaf should be drawn midway through his arm [*i.e.*, inside the bend of the elbow] ; and if this can be done without the defiling of his garments or his hair, then it is adjudged to be less than is right ; but otherwise it is judged sufficient." Or, again, when a serf is at work collecting sheaves, he must gather " fifty sheaves, each as great as he can drag under his arm while he holds the lap of his tunic in his hand." In another specification, he is allowed " to glean one handful which is called in the vulgar tongue *lashanwul* [leaze-handful]. The thirty salmon which the Northlode tenants owed yearly to Glastonbury kitchen must be " as thick at the tail as a man's wrist." The *medekniche* [mid-knee], on some Glastonbury manors, was " as much hay as the hayward can lift with his middle finger as far as his knees." More primitive still are some of the German measures. Many, as in England, offered sporting chances ; everything might depend on the question whether the load of wood could be dragged a certain distance from the forest before attracting attention ; whether the tenant has one foot or two within the moot-hall door before the moot has begun ; whether, when he has made up his mind to flit to another village, the steward can hold back his laden cart by the force of his single arm, or whether the tenant's oxen are strong enough to drag it on in the steward's despite. At Prüm, in 1640, if a malefactor on his way to prison " can spy that one of the lords [*i.e.*, monks of that great abbey] could be found outside the cloister ; and if the said malefactor can seize the aforesaid lord by his cowl, then shall he have six weeks and three days of freedom ; and this, as often as he can achieve the same." It is difficult to believe that the lords themselves did not take a sporting interest in their tenants' struggles, just as we know that our crusading knights earned the contempt of the dignified Moslems by setting old women to run a race for a pig.

G. G. Coulton, *The Mediæval Village*, pp. 35–48.

Historical Methods

(A)

He, Wolsey, was ordained priest on the title of his fellowship on 10 March, 1498 . . . (p. 12). He had started from Richmond on Tuesday, 5 April, and proceeded by way of Hendon, Rye House, Royston, and Huntingdon, spending a night at each, to Peterborough, where he remained from the 9th over Holy Week and Easter (17 April) until the 21st. On Maundy Thursday he washed the feet of fifty-nine* poor men and bestowed on each a royal largesse of " twelve pence in money, three ells of good canvass to make them shirtes, a paire of new shoes, a cast of red herrings, and three white herrings. . . .

A. F. Pollard, *Wolsey*, pp. 275–76 (1929).

* " Cavendish, p. 210. The number was supposed to denote the age of the person officiating, and this would place Wolsey's birth in 1470–1. Cavendish is now supposed to have been

(B)

Note (a).—On the Date of Wolsey's Birth

THE evidence consists in four points :

1. **The date of his ordination.**—Wolsey was ordained priest at Marlborough on the 10th March, 1498. It is to be presumed that his ordination would not have taken place till after his attainment of the canonical age ; he was not in early life of such importance or means as to procure a dispensation forestalling that date (nor was there likely to be any reason for such a dispensation). Now the canonical age is twenty-four. Wolsey, therefore, must have been born not *later* than early 1474 ; but may well have been born earlier.

mistaken and Wolsey to have been four years younger (*D.N.B.*). At Henry VIII.'s Maundy, however, in 1512 (8 April, *L.P.* ii., p. 1455) there were twenty-two beneficiaries, and on 28 March 1532 (*L.P.*, v. 863) there were forty-two, though Henry, having been born on 28 June 1491, was only twenty years and nine months old on the former, and forty on the latter occasion. Similarly on 8 April 1531 there were forty-one beneficiaries and each received 41d. (*ibid.* v., p. 325). The number taken for Maundy purposes seems to have been the number of years, incomplete as well as complete, in which the benefactor had lived. Wolsey's number of fifty-nine is therefore not incompatible with his having been born as late as 24 March 1472 (-73). He would thus, in April 1530, have lived in fifty-nine years, although he was only fifty-seven years and eleven months old. Giustiniani, reporting to the Venetian senate on 9 Oct. 1519, says Wolsey was ' about 46 years old,' which gives the same result. The abbot of Winchcombe's letter of 26 Aug. 1514 (*L.P.* i., 3925) on which the *D.N.B.* relies for Wolsey's birth in 1474–5 because it congratulates him on becoming archbishop before he was forty, must be discounted by its flattering implication that archbishops at forty were as rare as bishops, created at sixty or seventy, were common.''

2. The ceremony of April 14, 1530.—Maundy Thursday of the year 1530 fell upon April 14. On that day the number of those who benefited from the special alms allotted by Wolsey on the day was fifty-nine. Now it was the custom of kings and other great people who gave such largesse to a number of poor men every Maundy Thursday to make the number of the beneficiaries correspond to the age of the donor. The year was counted at that time from one Lady Day (25th March) to another, and the years enumerated were charitably estimated at the maximum ; that is, not the total amount of completed years the donor had lived but the total numbers of years *in which* he had lived : allowing Wolsey to have been born some time before Lady Day, 1473, but after Lady Day, 1472, he would thus have lived on April 14, 1530, *in* fifty-nine years, though he had only lived fifty-seven completed years.

3. Of less value but worth mentioning is a rough estimate written by Giustiniani on October 9, 1519, which says that Wolsey was then " about " forty-six years of age. A man born in late 1472 or early 1473 would, in October, 1519, have been drawing on to his forty-sixth birthday. This confirms point 2. Giustiniani was in a position to hear precise details, and of a character to note them exactly.

4. There is, indeed, an indication which would advance the date of his birth by at least a year, but it is too vague to outweigh the more precise evidence I have just given. It is an allusion by the Abbot of Winchcombe on August 6, 1514, saying that Wolsey at that date was under forty.

That would put the birth after August 6, 1474, but it is not a precise reference.

I conclude, therefore, for some date between 25th March, 1472, and 25th March, 1473, with a probability for an earlier rather than a later date in these twelve months.

HILAIRE BELLOC, *Wolsey*, (1930), p. 291.

The Use of Sources

IT is perhaps an inevitable result of the fact that economic history has been to such a great extent written by legal historians, that the medieval peasant is usually considered primarily in relation to his lord. The profusion of manorial documents and the fact that all we know of medieval farming is concerned (save by implication) with demesne farming have led to the same result. Yet the peasant was not only the inhabitant of a manor (and the manorial hold over him was often loose enough); he was a villager, the member of a community with a close and active life of its own. It was this village community which made rules for the common routine of husbandry, into which lord no less than tenant had to fit. Occasionally its regulations for such matters as the harvest are found enrolled upon court rolls; more often there have survived its customary rules for the use of forest and waste; and these are of great interest where there was an intercommoning of several vills over the same land, and often a *Markgenossenschaft*, with its own officials elected by the constituent villages to enforce the agreed regulations. The lords steadily encroached upon these organizations in the course of time, but they played an important part in rural life, and many of their regulations may be read in the German *Weistümer*.

The religious, the social, the family life of the villager all elude the historian who confines his attention to estate books and manorial documents, save in so far as court rolls throw their light on his less reputable moments, his often sanguinary feuds and hues and cries, his burglaries, and his daughter's peccadilloes. But there is ample other material from which to reconstruct it. Contemporary literature is rich in pictures of village life. What a familiar collection of types—*mutatis mutandis* still to be found in the countryside—is assembled in the thirteenth-century French *lai*, which prefaces " a rhymed octosyllabic curse " of peculiar force and comprehensiveness with a description of the twenty-three types of *vilains* to be stricken by it. There is the headman who announces feast days under the elm tree in front of the church, and the pious villagers who sit with the clerks and turn over the book of hours for them, and who carry the cross and the holy water in procession. There is the surly vinedresser who will not point out the way to travellers ; and the grumbler, who sits before his cottage door on Sundays and mocks the passers-by, and if he sees a gentleman coming along with a hawk on his wrist, he says, " Ho, that screech-owl will get a hen to eat to-night that would have given my children their bellyful ; " and there is the embittered fellow who hates God, Holy

Church, and the gentry. There is the accommodating ass (Vilain Asnin) who carries the cakes and wine to the feast, and if the weather is fine he carries his wife's cloak too, but if it is wet he strips himself to his breeches and covers her up. There is the country bumpkin, who goes to Paris and stands in front of Notre Dame, gaping up at the kings and saying, " Look, there's Pepin ! There's Charlemagne ! " while a pickpocket cuts his purse behind. There is the village leader, who speaks for the others to the bailiff, and says, " Sir, in my grandfather's and great-grandfather's time, our cows used to go in that meadow and our sheep in that copse," and so gains a hundred sous for the villeins. There are also the miser ; and the poacher who leaves his work at morn and eve to steal his lord's conies ; and the " cowled vilain, that is the poor married clerk who goes to work with the other vilains " ; and the wood-gatherer, who brings his load in backwards because his cottage door is so low ; and the marl-spreader, who upsets the last cartload over himself, " and he lies there and does not trouble the graveyard." Finally, there is " Vilain Graft, to wit he that taketh a gentlewoman to wife, even as a garden pear is grafted on a wild pear tree, or a cabbage or a turnip," a witness to the fact that in France, at least, rich peasants occasionally married above them. Similar pictures are to be found in the *fabliaux*, and they abound, likewise, in German and English literature. Meier Helmbrecht's family ; Chaucer's " povre widwe somdel stope in age," in whose yard dwelt Chantecler and Pertelote, that incomparable pair ; the village taverns in *Piers Plowman* and *The Tunnyng of Elynour Rummynge* (genre pictures as robust and redolent of the soil as Breughel's paintings); all these linger in the memory. Langland's great epic, indeed, is a whole gallery of peasant types, from the labourers who deigned not to dine on bacon and last night's vegetables, but must have hot fried fish to " the wo of these women that wonyeth in cotes " and the poor man's pride that will not let his neighbours see his need. This last passage—too well known for quotation—is equalled in pathos only by the poignant vignette in *Pierce the Plowman's Crede*, which shows the poor peasant and his wife plowing, with their little babe in a crumb-bowl at the end of the acre, and two-year-old twins tumbling beside it, all crying one cry, " a careful note." One is re-minded of the sentence, so significant and so devoid of sympathy, in Pelagius' *De Planctu Ecclesiae*, where he sets forth, among the sins of the peasant folk, that " they often abstain from knowing their own wives lest children should be born, fearing that they could not bring up so many, under pretext of poverty."

Another particularly valuable source of evidence for medieval village life, in its non-manorial aspects, is to be found in certain ecclesiastical documents, more particularly in those dealing with the parochial visitations, which took place from time to time. Records of several of such visitations have survived, notably those of four Norman parishes made by the Abbot of Cerisy's Official in the fourteenth century and those made by the Archdeacon of Josas in the Île de France between 1458 and 1470, both of which are particularly valuable in covering a number of consecutive years. The picture which they give of village life, with its immorality and violence and dilapidation, is a sombre one, and has sometimes been ascribed in part to the effect of the Hundred Years' War upon the countryside. That effect is, indeed, marked in the Josas series, a picture of desolation relieved only by the care with which, in place after place, the people are made to elect a village midwife, who is then sworn and licensed by the archdeacon. Nevertheless the general impression derived from those Cerisy visitations which belong to the period before the war is not very different from that derived from the later reports, although it is undeniably less gloomy, and there is much in common between both the Cerisy and the Josas series, and the reports of the visitations of the diocese of Hereford in 1397, which have recently come to light.

These Hereford returns give a picture of English village life, which is unsurpassed by that to be obtained from any other class of record. Here parish after parish is unrolled, with its superstitions, manners, morals, its village quarrels, and its relations with the church. It is the border country, where Welsh and English mingle, and occasionally the parson does not understand the language of his flock, as they complain. They are, indeed, nothing loath to complain of their parson if they have anything against him. The vicar of Eardisley is at feud with the whole parish; he has failed to supply a parish clerk, and his two maid-servants ring the bells and help him in the celebration of Mass, and his relations with them are gravely suspect ; several men have died without the last sacrament by his default, and when he was burying one John Boly in the churchyard, he said publicly in the hearing of those present, " Lie you there, excommunicate ! " He refuses to give the sacrament at Easter to the labourers of the parish, unless they agree with him for a tithe of their wages, and would not absolve a certain woman after confession unless she gave him 12d. towards the repair of the church books, so that she went into Hereford to get herself shriven. The church is befouled with flax and hemp, and he is a common trader in corn and other goods, and a usurer. *Differuntur omnia contravencia Vicarii sub spe concordie*, runs a note in the Register ; but the hope seems faint. Even when Hodge had no complaint against his parson, he was not a particularly devout son of the Church. He grumbled over mortuaries and tithes, tried to evade his turn to provide the *panis benedictus*, and was reported for not coming to church on Sundays or for working in the fields on holy days. Nevertheless the church was obviously the centre of village life. There the people went to be christened, married, and buried. They might or might not learn something of the truths of religion from their priest, but they got a rough familiarity with the lives of the saints and with the Bible from statue or storied capital or from wall-paintings, St. Christopher opposite the door to befriend the traveller, the Last Judgment over the chancel, and the Virgin in her lady chapel at the side. Nor did the people only use

the church for their devotions ; they were apt to
do their buying and selling in the porch, and the
priest himself sometimes stored and even threshed
his grain there. The churchyard, too, was a
convenient open space for village festivities. This
was well and good if a miracle play came round,
which might be considered edifying, but the fairs
which grew up round the churches were apt to
encroach on the churchyards, to the wrath of
ecclesiastical authorities, and sometimes the people
came there for dances and revels (pp. 740–43).

.   .   .   .

Such were the main features of peasant life and
rural conditions during the last four centuries of
the Middle Ages. From his contemporaries, or
at least from those whose opinions have come
down to us, the peasant received but little
appreciation. Clerkly writers scorned him, and
he was the butt of many half-proverbial rhymes
and epigrams. " Servi qui non timent, tument " ;
" rustica gens optima flens, pessima gaudens " ;
" oignez vilain, il vous poindra, poignez vilain il
vous oindra " ; " Knechte schlagen wenn sie
nicht zagen " ; " Der Bauer ist an Ochsen statt,
nur dass er keine Hörner hat." Very few are the
writers who suggest that villein is as villein does,
and express any sympathy for the hard lot of
those who labour in the fields. . . . It is not until
the later Middle Ages that there appears the
idealized peasant type, and the mystical exaltation
of manual labour performed not by monk but by
husbandman. Yet these inarticulate and despised
masses had two achievements to their credit,
which are worthy to be set beside the greatest

works of art and literature and government produced by the Middle Ages. They fed and colonized Europe; and slowly, painfully, laboriously they raised themselves from serfdom to freedom, laying hands as they did so upon a good proportion of that land which they loved with such a passionate and tenacious devotion (pp. 749–50).

> EILEEN E. POWER, " Peasant Life and Rural Conditions " (c. 1100 to c. 1500), *Cambridge Mediæval History*, VII., 716–50.

Original Texts

NEARLY all the present tendencies in the study of the Middle Ages are forms of one fruitful interest —the collection and criticism of original texts. It would be easy to discuss a number of subjects with which medievalists are especially preoccupied, and to say that these represent the trend of present learning. There is, for example, administrative history. There is the scattered work, which as it increases is gradually finding a unity of its own, upon the development of medieval thought and learning, revealed by scores of forgotten theologians, canonists, preachers, and moralists. There is the investigation, of which the work of Konrad Burdach and his school is a fine example, into the relations between chancery practice, political and ecclesiastical propaganda, and the art of writing ; the work which shows how poets and dreamers, humanists and political thinkers made themselves felt by way of the notarial art. There is the analysis of economic forces, the growth of credit, the use of instruments of exchange, the elaborate social expedients devised to meet the dangers of shipping and overseas trade, the effects of papal finance, the interplay of money payments and payments in kind. All these express tendencies in modern scholarship, and other examples could be given from the history of art and literature. It is possible to go further and to deduce from these tendencies some broad generalizations about the reactions of the modern or contemporary mind against traditional methods of regarding history. Yet, for every man or woman who is influenced by reactions of this kind, there is always another man or woman who is not. Beyond all these, and underlying all the work most characteristic of our time, is the interest in texts. When historical students get together they tend to talk about texts and the problems suggested by the study of texts ; where are they, what is happening to the manuscripts, what provision should be made for their safe-keeping, how ought we to edit them, what is the bearing of the un-published upon the published texts, is the record or the literary text the more valuable ? and so on. The old subjects of discussion tend to be left to debating societies, college essays, and examination papers. . . . Just as the study in combination of sculptural design, illuminated manuscripts, jewel work, and literary symbolism has broken new ground in the history of art and architecture, so the comparative study of texts, brought together with an intelligent (not a capricious) disregard of the limits set by artificial divisions, is throwing fresh light upon medieval society. It does not matter whether the text directly under consideration is a Pipe Roll or a passage in Geoffrey of Monmouth, a charter or a lecture in moral theology. The relevant texts, required in elucidation, may be few or many, but the alert appreciation of them must be there. We profit from a competent editor of an Assize Roll just as we profit from, let us say, M. Lot's analysis of the prose Lancelot.

F. M. POWICKE, " The Recent Trend of Medieval Historical Studies " (*History*, April 1932, pp. 1–2).

IV

RETROSPECT

What they undertook to do
They brought to pass.

W. B. Yeats.

SOME MODERN HISTORIANS

Bishop Stubbs, the Complete Historian

NO other Englishman has so completely displayed to the world the whole business of
the historian from the winning of the raw material
to the narrating and generalizing. We are taken
behind the scenes and shown the ropes and
pulleys ; we are taken into the laboratory and
shown the unanalysed stuff, the retorts and test-
tubes ; or rather we are allowed to see the organic
growth of history in an historian's mind and are
encouraged to use the microscope. This " practical demonstration," if we may so call it, of the
historian's art and science from the preliminary
hunt for manuscripts, through the work of collation and filiation and minute criticism, onward to
the perfected tale, the eloquence and the reflections, has been of incalculable benefit to the
cause of history in England and far more effective
than any abstract discourse on methodology could
be. In this respect we must look to the very
greatest among the Germans to find the peers of
Dr. Stubbs, and we must remember that a Mommsen's productive days are not cut short by a
bishopric. The matter that lay in the hands of

our demonstrator was, it is true, medieval, and the method was suited to the matter, but in those famous introductions are lessons of patient industry, accurate statement, and acute but wary reasoning which can be applied to all times and to every kind of evidence. The very mingling of small questions with questions that are very large is impressive. The great currents in human affairs, and even " the moral government of the universe," were never far from the editor's mind when he was determining the relation between two manuscripts or noting a change of hand, and then if he turned for a while to tell big history it was with a mind that still was filled to the full with tested facts and sifted evidence.

F. W. MAITLAND, *Collected Papers*, III., p. 498.

Lord Acton

HE believed, that as an investigator of facts the historian must know no passion, save that of a desire to sift evidence ; and his notion of this sifting was of the remorseless scientific school of Germany, which sometimes, perhaps, expects more in the way of testimony than human life affords. At any rate, Acton demanded that the historian must never misconceive the case of the adversaries of his views, or leave in shade the faults of his own side. But, on the other hand, when he comes to interpret facts or to trace their relation, his views and even his temperament will affect the result. It is only the barest outline that can be quite effective. In Acton's view the historian as investigator is one thing, the historian as judge another. In an early essay on Döllinger he makes a distinction of this kind. The reader must bear it in mind in considering Acton's own writing. Some of the essays . . . and still more the lectures, are anything but colourless ; they show very distinctly the predilections of the writer, and it is hardly conceivable that they should have been written by a defender of absolutism, or even by an old-fashioned Tory. What Acton really demanded was not the academic aloofness of the pedant who stands apart from the strife of principles, but the honesty of purpose which " throws itself into the mind of one's opponents, and accounts for their mistakes," giving their case the best possible colouring. For, to be sure of one's ground, one must meet one's adversaries' strongest arguments, and not be content with merely picking holes in his armour. Otherwise one's own belief may be at the mercy of the next clever opponent. The reader may doubt how far Acton succeeded in his own aim, for there was a touch of intolerance in his hatred of absolutism, and he believed himself to be divided from his ecclesiastical and political foes by no mere intellectual difference but by a moral cleavage. Further, his writing is never half-hearted. His convictions were certitudes based on continual reading and reflection, and admitting in his mind of no qualification. He was eminently a Victorian in his confidence that he was right. He had none of the invertebrate tendency of mind which thinks it is impartial merely because it is undecided and regards the judicial attitude as that which refrains from judging. Acton's was not a doubting mind. If he now and then suspended his judgment, it was an act of deliberate choice, because he had made up his mind that the matter could not be decided, not because he could not decide to make up his mind. Whether he was right or wrong, he always knew what he thought, and his language was as exact an expression of his meaning as he could make it. It was true that his subtle and far-sighted intelligence makes his style now and then like a boomerang, as when he says of Ranke's method " it is a discipline we shall all do well to adopt, and also do well to relinquish." Indeed, it is hardly possible to read a single essay without observing this marked characteristic. He has been called a " Meredith turned historian," and that there is truth in this judgment any one who sees at once the difficulty and the suggestiveness of his reviews can bear witness. He could hardly write the briefest note without stamping his personality upon it and exhibiting the marks of a very complex culture. But the main characteristic of his style is that it represents the ideals of a man to whom every word was sacred. Its analogies are rather in sculpture than painting. Each paragraph, almost every sentence, is a perfectly chiselled whole, impressive by no brilliance or outside polish, so much as by the inward intensity of which it is the symbol. Thus his writing is never fluent or easy, but it has a moral dignity rare and unfashionable.

Acton, indeed, was by no means without a gift of rhetoric, and . . . there is ample evidence of a power of handling words which should impress a popular audience. It is in gravity of judgment and in the light he can draw from small details that his power is most plainly shown. On the other hand, he had a little of the scholar's love of clinging to the bank, and, as the notes to his " Inaugural " show, he seems at times too much disposed to use the crutches of quotation to prop up positions which need no such support. It was of course the same habit—the desire not to speak before he had read everything that was relevant, whether in print or manuscript—that hindered so severely his output. His projected *History of Liberty* was, from the first, impossible of achievement. It would have required the intellects of Napoleon and Julius Cæsar combined, and the lifetime of the patriarchs, to have executed that project as Acton appears to have planned it. A *History of Liberty*, beginning with the ancient world and carried down to our own day, to be based entirely upon original sources, treating both of the institutions which secured it, the persons who fought for it, and the ideas which expressed it, and taking note of all that scholars had written about every several portion of the subject, was and is beyond the reach of a single man. Probably towards the close of his life Acton had felt this. The *Cambridge Modern History*, which required the co-operation of so many specialists, was to him really but a fragment of this great project.

The History of Freedom, by Lord Acton (ed. J. N. Figgis and R. V. Laurence), pp. xxxiii–xxxvi.

Frederick William Maitland

As an historian he was eminently a "path-
finder," and has probably done more to revolu-
tionize our ideas of English origins than any one,
except Stubbs and, possibly, Liebermann. His
interests were precisely opposite to those of
Creighton. To the latter the personal side of
history strongly appealed, and while there is no
trace in either writer of any striving after what is
picturesque and dramatic, it is evident that the
analysis of character takes a foremost place in the
method of Creighton, while it is the development
of institutions that normally interests Maitland.
The latter cares for the structure of civilized life,
its juridical skeleton and economic basis; the
former for the men who work upon the structure,
for the manipulators of institutions, for the diplo-
matist and the statesman. Not that Maitland
is ever dry, or that Creighton is always vivid.
Both are alike in this, that they enlarged the
horizons of all cultivated Englishmen. Creighton's
interest was primarily European, and even Italian;
his book, incidentally, is a better history of the
Renaissance than the pretentious volubility of
Symonds. It is the theatre of European statecraft
at the period of transition from the dream of
mediæval unity to the reality of modern national-
ism that Creighton loved to gaze upon, and so to
raise his readers above the narrow and insular
view of history which is characteristic of so many
Englishmen.

Maitland had a similar feeling, in spite of the

fact that his work lay almost exclusively in the origins of English legal and constitutional life. I heard him criticize a scheme for historical teaching on the ground that it was " far too English." He desired that youths should be trained to see history from a standpoint not of their own nation, which is comparatively easy to attain, but of the best science of Germany, and perhaps even more of France. For although Maitland's studies were emphatically directed to find by " slow degrees the thoughts of our forefathers," " to think once more their common thoughts about common things," he knew very well that this would not be achieved without an endeavour to correlate the development of this country to that of others in Western Europe, insisting not only on the differences, which are superficial, but on the resemblances, which, at least up to the fourteenth century, are essential and profound. Creighton and Maitland and Acton were in fact at work on one problem—the development of the modern Western mind and its relation to the sources from which it had proceeded. Only Creighton envisaged the problem from the standpoint of the statesman-ecclesiastic, Maitland from that of a trained lawyer, and Acton from that of a political and ethical philosopher. All were alike in that their method was eminently that of historically-minded thinkers ; but they differed in standpoint, in opinion, and to some extent in the material each made his own. Maitland—to return to him—more than any one else is responsible for the annihilation of what may be called the lawyer's view of history, which dates everything from the thirteenth century, and regards the reign of Henry II. as equally with that of Henry I. in legal twilight. Even before Maitland it had dawned upon a few legal minds that there were great men before Stephen Langton, and that a theory of English land-law and the courts which went little further back than Edward I. was not likely to be adequate (except, of course, for the practice of the courts). Just as it needed Freeman, with all his faults, to induce the ordinary historical reader to believe that anything really happened before 1066, so it needed Maitland, with all his genius, to break down the even more intolerable tyranny of insuler jurists, and to limit the empire of Coke. There are few passages more illuminating, not only for the English student, but for all those interested in the growth of mediæval institutions on the ruins of the Roman Empire, than the few introductory pages on the nature of feudalism in *The History of English Law* (Vol. I., pp. 66–73). The writer, who heard this, or most of it, delivered as a lecture in that small room at Downing on a dark autumn afternoon to a yet smaller audience, is not likely to forget the impression then made.

This brings me to one point about Maitland which might be otherwise neglected—his characteristics as a lecturer. If the main impression given by Creighton was that of intellectual versatility and alertness, of the duty of thinking things out, the main impression of Maitland was that of the paramount importance of what he was talking about. His style was and is like that of no one else, compact of extraordinary Biblical and other archaisms, intensely individual, vivid, and striking, packed with allusions, sparkling with humour, and suggesting even more than it stated—the very opposite of the matter-of-fact, unadorned narrative of Creighton as an historian. It was a style like the portrait of Monna Lisa, which all the thoughts and experiences of the world seemed to have moulded, and it had, whether delivered or written, an extraordinary quality, almost unique among historians—that of reproducing the atmosphere of the time he was discussing. It was not descriptive or picturesque in the ordinary sense. There was neither the hardness nor the brilliancy, still less the partisanship of Macaulay in Maitland's mind. But just as he left his hearers under the impression that there was only one thing worth living for—the study of twelfth-century law—as he discoursed in his vibrating and nervous tones (for he was nervous to the last), so his writing serves to bring before us the mental atmosphere of the men he talks of with a reality quite unlike that of the narrative historian, and quite different from the memoir-writer. Perhaps it was best expressed once in the phrase of Mr. Andrew Lang, that he turned flashes of electric light on his subject.

Maitland, in fact, is to the ordinary historian what Mr. Sargent is to the ordinary portrait painter. The genius for life is perhaps the best name for the characteristic which makes them both so different from other men, which marks their quality and limits as well as expands their powers. Stubbs is a great historian, but he tells us of a dog that remains dead ; Froude is a great dramatist, but he delights us with the tragedy of personality. Macaulay paints pictures. Maitland shows us life, and not the lives of statesmen merely, but of human beings. Other men know and we learn from them. Maitland saw, and we learn more from him ; only what he sees is not the dress, the buildings, and the accessories of life, but the inner world of thought and feeling, " the common thoughts of our fathers about common things." This is what I mean by likening him to Sargent, from whose pictures the genius of the fevered world he portrays will look out for ever, for a new Maitland to interpret in an age yet to come.

J. N. FIGGIS, *Churches in the Modern State,* App. II., " Three Cambridge Historians : Creighton, Maitland, and Acton," pp. 227–65.

The Great Historians

HISTORY should not lose touch with its own past. The works of great historians of former times ought to be known not only by name but by use. They should not always be relegated to the dust heap, because on certain points they have been supplemented or corrected by works of smaller intellectual power. Students of English literature are not in the habit of confining their reading to the neo-Georgian poets ; and although history is less perennial than poetry, it is in its higher manifestation not so ephemeral as some people are inclined to suppose. We historians also have our heritage, not least in England. The doctrine of the permanent value of great historians was finely enforced by Bury when he re-edited

Gibbon, to help keep him in use for modern students.

Since history consists not only in collecting facts about the past, but in thinking about them, old fashions of historical thought are not to be neglected. They often serve as a useful corrective to the fashion of our own age, which is not the quintessence of all that has gone before, but merely the latest mode, with its strong points, certainly, but also, we may be sure, with its weak spots as well. Besides some great names that I have already mentioned, there are historians and biographers, such as Sorel, Lecky, Creighton, Symonds, Dicey, Gardiner, Morley, Jessopp, Parkman, Motley, Ranke, Gregorovius, Taine, Tocqueville, Guizot, and many more, who have things to suggest to us, all the more valuable because we may not have them from contemporaries. The succession of attitudes adopted by the men of the eighteenth and nineteenth centuries towards the past is in itself no unimportant part of history.

Among books written before the eighteenth century, in days when the study of the past laboured under great disadvantages, the historical literature of most educational value for us is, perhaps, the contemporary memoir of passing events, such as Burnet and Clarendon, de Commines and Froissart. Can a man be said to have had a liberal education in English history if he has never read some, at least, of the nobler passages in Clarendon? And those magnificent political controversies, if we give them no higher title, conducted by Milton and Burke, are part of the young history student's birthright as an Englishman ; to know something of them, he may well be expected to spare a few hours from learning so many more clauses of broken treaties out of textbooks.

G. M. TREVELYAN, *The Present Position of History,* pp. 21–23.

George Unwin

UNWIN's discoveries, like those of other historians, will be superseded by the work of later students. His most characteristic contribution will not. For it consisted, not in the specific additions which he made to the knowledge of particular problems or periods, but in his emphasis on certain simple, yet fundamental, truths which are commonly forgotten. He did more than any other English scholar to enlarge the horizon of economic history. He changed its focus, brought new ranges of phenomena into the field of vision, and recast the categories applied to the interpretation of social development.

At the beginning of the present century, economic history was still something of a parvenu in England. Parvenus are apt to ape the costume of the society into which they seek admission. Inevitably, though unconsciously, economic historians had tended to borrow the assumptions of their colleagues, the political historians—to plan their work on lines of national development, to put the activities of governments in the forefront of the picture, to see the landmarks of economic progress and rivalries of States. The example of German scholars, and a not unnatural reaction against what seemed an artificial divorce of economics from politics in the work of some English political economists, strengthened the same tendency. Dr. Cunningham, who had done more than any other English student to map out the field, had made the transition from State-control to a policy of *laissez-faire* the basis of his scheme. Lesser writers followed his example, and strung an assortment of economic facts on a political framework.

The effect of Unwin's work as a historian was to undermine this tradition among all who came under his influence. His leading idea was to present an interpretation of social development in which emphasis should be transferred from organization to growth—from the policy of States to the enterprise of individuals and the rise of different types of corporate association. He altered the perspective of economic history, freed it from much conventional lumber, and gave it a new objective and centre of interest. He found it strongly biassed towards politics. He left it with a bias towards sociology.

His starting point was the error which springs from the view that history is past politics, and the necessity of reducing to humble dimensions the contribution to civilization to be ascribed to the State. "The essential element in my philosophy," he wrote to a friend, " is my relegation of politics to an entirely subordinate plane of spiritual reality. The study of history has confirmed this valuation, and all my teaching is based upon it. I think the part played by State power in history has been very largely evil. The State provides channels for the overflow of the evil will-to-power of men acting collectively, and these channels must be stopped before political action can be healthy." He found it as difficult to believe that far-reaching changes had their cause, except in a purely formal sense, in the policy of governments, as Tolstoi that the invasion of Russia took place because Napoleon ordered it.

The illusion, he would argue, that the history of man is the history of man's political organization, and that the exercise of power by national States has been a principal instrument of social progress, is easily intelligible. The mind instinctively seeks a continuous chain of causation in history, and, in following the thread of governmental policy, it seems to come nearer than elsewhere to grasping it. In reality, however, half, and the better half, of human life is concerned with interests which derive their vitality, not from political organization, but from the spontaneous association of men for mutual aid, for economic effort and intercourse, for culture and worship. The web of civilization is woven, not by governments, but by individuals, and the threads which compose it are not the formal bonds which stretch from sovereign to subject, but a thousand delicate filaments spun by the creative energy of countless spirits. Progress in the arts which enrich and ennoble life has taken place, not because of the growth in the powers of States, but independently of them. Too often, indeed, it has taken place in spite of them. For the beginning of wisdom is to recognize that destructive and constructive forces interact in social development. There is an element in human affairs which might be called satanic. A not inconsiderable proportion of the episodes which popular history sets in a high light—war, the conquest and government of subject races, international rivalry and commercial *Machtpolitik* —are morbid phenomena : phases, not in the advance of civilization, but in its breakdown ; a record of waste and futility and crime, disguised as constructive achievements by the romanticism of writers and the credulity of public opinion.

A great part of history consists of such relapses. To ignore them, or to conceal their true nature, is the sin against the Holy Ghost. It is to lead mankind to believe that it can be strengthened by feeding on poison. So the historian must investigate them, as the student of medicine investigates cholera or cancer ; the special function, indeed, of the economic historian is to reveal the conditions from which such phenomena emerge and the effects which they produce. But the life of an organism is not to be explained by its pathology. Political societies are secondary, societies based on kinship, on economic needs, on culture and religion, are primary. The fundamental aspect of history is the growth, not of States, but of communities transcending them. It is the rise of voluntary associations of ever greater variety and of ever widening range and inclusiveness. It is through a fuller appreciation of the part played in social development by these communities of life and work, of the causes which have produced them, the results which they have achieved, and the transformation through which they have passed, that the dangerous delusions fostered by a too exclusive preoccupation with political phenomena are most likely to be corrected. History, if it is to keep in touch with reality, must devote as much attention to the study of forms of social and economic organization as to that of political institutions. It must be social ; it must also be international. For the economic development of Europe is a single theme ; all nations have lent and all have borrowed ; and the civilization of each is a cosmopolitan creation to which all have contributed. The science which interprets it must be equally free from the limitations of nationality. It must be, " not the sacred egotism of nations projected into the past, but the history of the world told from the world's point of view."

These doctrines found expression in Unwin's criticisms upon conventional presentations of economic development, and in his own attempts to redress the balance. He thought that the treatment of the Middle Ages, with their wealth of corporate associations and with political interests in a subordinate position, had suffered less than that of later periods, but that, with the rise of national States and of international rivalries, a subtle distortion crept in, which threw much of the history of the last three centuries into a false perspective. His own exposition was intended to correct it, not by controversy, but by a readjustment of emphasis.

Its note was an insistence on the impersonal

aspects of history, as distinguished from governmental policies. In dealing with the period from the sixteenth to the eighteenth centuries, he dwelt at length on the increasing range and complexity of economic organization in credit, international trade, textiles, and mining, and gave a quite subordinate place to mercantilism, as a negative and restrictive factor which had its principal source, not in any deliberate plan of promoting economic progress, but in the fiscal exigencies of short-sighted and impecunious governments. Tudor paternalism was explained, not as a benevolent social policy, but as a belated attempt to crystallize decaying economic relationships, which was obsolete before it was formulated. Hawkins and Drake were presented, not as the pioneers of the British Empire, but as buccaneers who disorganized international economic relations by piracy on the high seas, and who, incidentally, made expansion more difficult by sapping its economic foundations. The commercial wars of the eighteenth century were dismissed as at once futile and immoral. Canada, he would argue, would have been British had Wolfe never fallen on the Heights of Abraham, for the British settlers in North America outnumbered the French before the Seven Years' War began, and were increasing in numbers far more rapidly. The significance of the Industrial Revolution he found in the growth of a vaster and more complex community, embracing an ever-increasing proportion of mankind in a single system of economic relations. His lectures on the nineteenth century gave much space to questions of the growth and movement of population, to the rise of new forms of association, and to the economic unification of the world after 1870.

. . . .

It is possible that he overshot the mark, and that his scepticism of the achievements of authority was exaggerated. It is possible, too, that in his distrust of the political leviathan, he sometimes forgot that there are economic monsters, which also are not without teeth and claws. But a bent stick needs an effort to straighten it, and most students both of history and of economics will sympathize with the realist who tilts at romance. In a world indifferent to the political applications of his favourite quotation from Voltaire—" It is certain that spells and incantations will destroy large flocks of sheep, provided that they are accompanied by sufficient doses of arsenic "—he thought it more important to explain the properties of arsenic than to appraise with nicety the merits of competing spells.

R. H. TAWNEY, *Studies in Economic History: The Collected Papers of George Unwin,* pp. lxi–lxvi (1927).

Thomas Frederick Tout

TOUT'S historical work speaks for itself. The great book upon which his fame will mainly rest is a positive and unadorned contribution to knowledge, so massive that none can fail to realize it, so intelligently related to the facts of life that none can afford to neglect it. But whatever he wrote—lectures, articles, reviews, text-books, treatises—was concrete, vigorous, unaffected, and direct, even conversational, its merits obvious, its blemishes unconcealed. His master, Stubbs, was the outstanding constructive force in the historical scholarship of his time, and Tout, perhaps even more than the more brilliant and versatile Maitland, carried on this positive and energetic tradition. No critic, knowing what Tout did, need have the slightest hesitation in admitting his defects. He lived in a generation of very fine medievalists. He did not possess the finished scholarship of this scholar, nor the acute penetration of that, nor the fastidious, remorseless pertinacity of a third. He was an untidy builder ; but he built, and his work stands, firm and four-square. He worked with a kind of deliberate fury, and very quickly, always going straight to the texts and manuscripts if he were engaged upon a piece of original work. He believed, and he insisted on this in advising his pupils, in mastering the published texts first and in reading them continuously as texts, not in consulting them as collections of raw material. He knew the pleasure of reading a chronicle in his easy chair. If he was not so thorough in his consideration of all the modern authorities, he knew where to look and rarely missed anything of significance. He wrote hard, not troubling much about form, but getting at the essentials with the pungent, vivid, direct, adjectival exuberance of his oral speech. His best writing, as in some of his published lectures (which remind one of Freeman), and in his survey of the character and policy of King Richard II., is very like his best speech. He was methodical in big rather than in small things, so that his work required drastic revision, a dreary task which taxed his patience. Hence he owed very much, during the preparation of the last volumes of his big book, to the expert and methodical scholarship of his secretary, Dr. Dorothy Broome, whose help received his warm and generous recognition.

. . . .

Tout's work illustrates a truth too often neglected, that good realistic history cannot be written unless the historian possesses a powerful and well-disciplined imagination. If we are conscious of seeing, as though for the first time, an old institution at work, or of understanding the significance of a group of apparently insignificant officials, it means that imaginative effort has given life to a mass of dreary details. This kind of imaginative faculty follows the facts ; it is not the same as the artistic faculty—a much more dangerous thing in the historian—by which impressions are consciously recreated in the writer's mind. Each involves effort, and each is fed by the wide human interests of the writer. Neither is capable of " dry-as-dust " history, for neither is remote from life. Both make demands upon the reader, but the reader's attention may wander, in the one case into misunderstanding, in the other into the realm of illusion. Tout, if he had ever cared to argue about it, would undoubtedly have agreed with a distinguished German contemporary that the science or learning of the romantic or of any other period of enlightenment was more important than its poetry. His work satisfied him in the way in which music or poetry satisfies other men. In this sense of satisfaction he was throughout consistent with himself. He could never quite understand the dissipation of interest which follows a divided allegiance. At Lampeter he was distressed when members of the staff absented themselves from a weekly social gathering started by themselves, and at Manchester I have seen him half-puzzled, half-indignant, if one of us deserted an historical conference for a concert. He had, of course, other strong interests of his own, especially in travel and archæology and literature. But he regarded these interests as relaxations which should never distract a man from the daily task. It was interesting to hear him talk about an old building, and he was at his happiest, on an historical excursion, when he was describing to a group of students, in his racy and gesticulating fashion, an antiquity like Whalley Abbey or Conisbrough Castle. He always made them feel its interest as an expression of history, and I fancy that he could never quite enjoy a beautiful thing for its own sake unless he knew something about it and had set it in its various periods. Æsthetic pleasure without such knowledge would have seemed amateurish to him. On the other hand he could find real enjoyment in things which the more conventional historical student overlooks or rejects. He took a childlike pleasure in tracing with his children, the courses of the wretched streams which trickle through the suburbs of Manchester to join the Mersey and the Irwell; and, with the imagination of the scholar, he saw in them the links with the past, when the marshy spaces were dotted with island hamlets, and Manchester was confined to the rocky triangle between the Irwell and the Irk. It was in this spirit of adventure, rejoicing in the details for the significance which could be found in them, that in later years he worked upon the problems of medieval administration. It is given to few men to feel, as the years close about them, the same zest in the bewildering contents of the Public Record Office as they felt in earlier days in exploring the antiquities of Gascony and Provence.

The *Chapters in the Administrative History of Medieval England* should be read in the spirit in which they were written. Tout was pursuing no learned by-paths. He was concerned to understand the methods of medieval government, and to adjust the generalizations of the constitutional historian to the salutary experience of men, great men and little men, ministers of state and clerks living their lives of routine among associations now long forgotten. He went back and appropriated the traditions of the great scholars of the seventeenth century, in whose time the medieval institutions of England were still at work, and in whose eyes the methods of chancery and exchequer practice, and the co-operation of the royal household with the state which it supervised, were still of obvious significance. And with opportunities for investigation greater than those open to Spelman and Prynne and Madox, he tried to work out in detail the interplay, from year to year, of administration and policy. The outcome is not all of equal value. It lacks proportion and some of it is not inspired ; but it is undoubedly one of the outstanding achievements of English historical learning.

F. M. POWICKE in *The Collected Papers of Thomas Frederick Tout*, I., pp. 20–24 (1932).

V

REVIEWING

Ile write, because Ile give
You.Criticks means to live :
For sho'd I not supply
The Cause, th' effect wo'd die.
Herrick.

293

THE REVIEWERS

THE practice of publishing in periodicals reviews of new books, is one of those blessings of civilization which were not known in the Middle Ages or in antiquity. It is usually, and I believe correctly, said to have begun with the French *Journal des Scavans* in 1665. What this journal provided met the needs of the reading public at that time so well that it was translated or imitated within a few years all over Europe. Early in the eighteenth century the custom had taken the place it still holds, and by the time of Dr. Johnson the two main kinds of reviewers, as we still know them, were easily distinguished. " The Critical Reviewers, I believe," Johnson said, " often review without reading the books through ; but lay hold of a topick and write chiefly from their own minds. The Monthly Reviewers are duller men, and are glad to read the books through." Though one of the writers of the *Critical Review* was Smollett, the great days of English reviewing had not yet come. It was in the early nineteenth century that the reviewer reached the height of his authority, and, on the other hand, became an object of frequent satire in verse and prose ; the *Edinburgh* was founded in 1802, and the *Quarterly* in 1809. The later development of reviewing in England, including that special branch of it which is our concern, is best understood if it is regarded as carrying on and modifying the tradition of that period.

.   .   .   .

The reviewer's task is to indicate what are the contents of a book and what he thinks of them, what the author attempted, how far the attempt was well-advised, and how far it succeeded. He may do more than this. There are some distinguished historians who try, whenever they write reviews, to include in them some positive original contribution to knowledge. There are even some whose learning is so great and so ready that they cannot write anything at all without illuminating the subject. It would be too much to expect this of reviewers in general, and a word of warning may even be uttered about the dangers of trying to imitate this admirable example. Occasionally really important discoveries announced in this incidental way have not attracted such wide attention as they deserved and have been forgotten, so that other inquirers had to make them afresh. It would have been better to keep them for some more ostentatious form of announcement. If the reviewer restricts himself to his narrower task, he has enough to do. Two small questions about this are sometimes discussed. Is it useful, first, to summarize the contents of the book? Summarizing is easier than criticism. It is a way of preserving neutrality and avoiding the expression of opinion, so that reviewers are often tempted to resort to it. There are some readers who find it very useful, though opinions differ about this, and many reviewers do not seem to know how much of the real work of a summary may be done far more briefly by a descriptive statement of a book's contents. Summarizing is sometimes, in these days of dear printing and paper, impossible unless something is sacrificed from the space given to criticism ; and if there must be a choice between the two, the latter, as being what the reader is less likely to be able to do for himself, should be preferred. The second question is how far a reviewer should point out and correct the mistakes in a book. Some reviewers regularly point out trivial misprints and slips, and nothing is more disappointing and irritating to an author than to be faced with a review consisting mainly of these pin-pricks. Sometimes they result from timidity ; some reviewers do not like to say that a book contains many misprints and small errors without enumerating enough to fortify the statement. A slightly different, but not more respectable, motive is the fear that the reviewer, if he does not notice them, may be supposed to have overlooked these errors. Where there is any doubt, it seems that the best guiding principle to take is the simple one that mistakes should be pointed out in such a way and with such an amount of detail as will best prevent a reader from being misled.

A more important formula, which is often useful to historical reviewers when doubts arise about the best way of going to work, is this, that the review of a book should above all indicate its place in the literature of the subject. The difference between the state of mind of the trained historian and that of the general reader is that the historian regards an historical source or study not as an isolated body of information, true or false, but as occupying its own place in a vast but not trackless or incoherent aggregate of books which together constitute what is known on the period or subject in question. What enables him to find his way about in this accumulation of materials is the double knowledge that every historical statement comes from somewhere, has had an original source, and can never by any subsequent process acquire any better title to belief than those sources had themselves, and that every historical book is to be regarded in its relation to the sources of the statements and judgments contained in it. What he specially wants to know about it is whether the author has used new materials or made new and more correct interpretations of old materials. If he has done either of these things, he has contributed to historical knowledge. If there is nothing new in the book it is of no historical value. Whether there is anything new and how much, and what it is, and how it affects what was previously known, are the main things which the student of history wishes to be told.

In conclusion I should like to continue the same line of thought by saying that no study can gain more from good reviewing than history. History is provided by a great army of workers, an army to which in a sense almost the whole population belongs, and the reviewer is one of the " pivotal " men in the organization. As everybody knows, the first step in giving the world its history is the selection of materials, and we all play a part in this selection, deciding what things are to be preserved and what are to go irretrievably to oblivion. When we fill up the counterfoils of cheques or destroy the envelopes of our morning mail we are giving or taking away materials which may or may not, as we then decide, be of use to historians. That is the first of many siftings, and to describe the entire machine would be to describe the world of living men. If we look at the whole available mass of information about the past, we see that there have been two kinds of choosing. Sometimes the selection has been deliberate, as when government departments decide which of their records to file and which to burn ; sometimes it has been quite haphazard. Much of it has been done by fire and earthquake and civil disturbance, and, of that part which has been done not by chance but by foresight, much has been for other needs than those of the historian. We owe a great deal to family pride in all ages ; we also owe much to the negligence of scavengers. The final stages of selection are always being done by historians and their readers, but the historian is only one of this imperfectly organized army in which book-sellers, librarians, publishers' readers, the makers of pulping machines, and thousands of others have their respective functions. The reviewer is a liaison officer between several of these groups. His work will contribute to decide not only who will buy or read a book, but also how far it will be accepted, what place will be assigned to it in the advance of historical studies. He works under conditions which make it likely that what he has written will not be consulted many years after he has written it. Not many reviews are collected and reprinted in book-form like those of the great masters. But even if reviews come low in what is, after all, never more than a relative scale of permanence, their work is not less important for that. The better it is done, indeed, the more quickly and finally it should be superseded. It turns the march of historians into the right roads and breaks up the ambushes of error ; but the sooner it is left behind, the more certain it is that the advance guard has gone forward.

> G. N. Clark, " Historical Reviewing " (in *Essays in History Presented to Reginald Lane Poole*, ed. H. W. C. Davis, pp. 115–26).

SELECT BIBLIOGRAPHY

ACTON, SIR JOHN, first Baron Acton of Aldenham [1834–
1902], sometime Regius Professor of Modern History in
the University of Cambridge.

For life and list of writings see *Dictionary National
Biography, Supp.* (1901–11), and W. A. Shaw, *A
Bibliography of the Historical Works* (1903). Critical
estimates in J. Bryce, *Studies in Contemporary Biography* ; J. N. Figgis, *Churches in the Modern State* ;
and introductions to *Lectures in Modern History* and
The History of Freedom. A full length study of Acton's
work is Ulrich Noack, *Geschichtswissenschaft und Wahr-
heit* and *Katholizität und Geistesfreiheit* (Frankfurt, 1935,
1936). Some of Acton's best work in *Lectures on
Modern History*, ed. R. V. Lawrence and J. N. Figgis
(1912) ; *The History of Freedom and Other Essays*
(1907) ; *Historical Essays and Studies* (1908) ; *Lectures
on the French Revolution* (1910).

ALLEN, PERCY S. [1869–1933], President of Corpus Christi
College, Oxford.

His life-work, an edition of the letters of Erasmus
(*Opus Epistolarum Des. Erasmi Roterodami* (1906–28)
is one of the great achievements of English scholarship
in this century. For an account of his work see
H. W. Garrod, *Percy Stafford Allen* (1934) ; H. de Vocht,
In Memoriam : Percy Stafford Allen (1934). Some of his
best papers have been collected in *The Age of Erasmus*
(1914) and *Erasmus Lectures and Wayfaring Sketches*
(1934).

BIRRELL, AUGUSTINE [1850–1933], literary critic.

For some historical essays see *The Collected Essays and
Addresses of the Rt. Hon. Augustine Birrell, 1880–1920*,
3 vols. (1922).

BURY, JAMES BAGNELL [1861–1927], Regius Professor of Modern History in the University of Cambridge.

For life and bibliography consult N. H. Baynes, *A Bibliography of the Works of J. B. Bury, Compiled with a Memoir* (1929). For Bury's ideas on the scope and method of history, *Selected Essays of J. B. Bury* (ed. H. W. V. Temperley, 1930) and a review by R. C. Collingwood in *English Historical Review* (xlvi., 461–5). Some of the more general of Bury's works are *A History of the Later Roman Empire from Arcadius to Irene*, 2 vols. (1889) ; *A History of the Eastern Roman Empire from the Fall of Irene to the Accession of Basil I.* (1912) ; *The History of the Later Roman Empire from the Death of Theodosius I. to the Death of Justinian*, 2 vols. (1923) ; " The Ottoman Conquest " (in *Cambridge Modern History*, Vol. I., chap. 3. (1902)) ; *A History of Freedom of Thought* (1914) ; *The Idea of Progress* (1920).

CLAPHAM, JOHN HAROLD, Professor of Economic History in the University of Cambridge.

Works include *The Woollen and Worsted Industries* (1907) ; *The Abbé Sieyès* (1912) ; *The Economic Development of France and Germany, 1815–1914* (1921) ; *An Economic History of Modern Britain* (1926, 1932) ; *The Study of Economic History* (1929).

CLARK, GEORGE NORMAN, Chichele Professor of Economic History in the University of Oxford.

For his inaugural lecture on economic history see " The Study of Economic History," in *History*, N.S. XVII. (July 1932), pp. 97–110. Other works, *The Seventeenth Century* (1929) and *The Later Stuarts, 1660–1714* (Oxford History of England, 1934).

COULTON, GEORGE GORDON, University Lecturer in English in the University of Cambridge.

Profound respect for the range of Dr. Coulton's knowledge has been mingled with criticism of his historical method—see *e.g.* F. M. Powicke's " critical appreciation rather than an attack " in " The Historical Method of Mr. Coulton," in *History*, N.S. VIII. (January 1924), pp. 256–68, and Coulton's defence in " Two Ways of History," *ibid*. IX. (April 1924), pp. 1–12. His works include : *Five Centuries of Religion*, Vol. I. (1923),

II. (1927), III. (1936) ; *The Mediæval Village* (1925) ; *Ten Mediæval Studies* (1930) ; *Art and the Reformation* (1928).

CREIGHTON, MANDELL [1843–1901], historian and bishop successively of Peterborough and London.

For life and works consult L. Creighton, *Life and Letters of Mandell Creighton*, 2 vols. (1904), and W. A. Shaw, *A Bibliography of the Historical Works* (1903). See also J. N. Figgis, *Churches in the Modern State*. Most important of Creighton's books are *The History of the Papacy During the Reformation, 1378–1527*, 6 vols. (1882–1894) ; *Cardinal Wolsey* (1888) ; *The Early Renaissance in England* (1895) ; *Queen Elizabeth* (1896).

DAVIS, HENRY WILLIAM CARLESS [1874–1918], Regius Professor of Modern History in the University of Oxford.

For life, essays, and bibliography see *H. W. C. Davis : A Memoir* (ed. J. R. H. Weaver and A. L. Poole, 1933). Works include *Charlemagne* (1900) ; *England under the Normans and Angevins* (1905) ; *Mediæval Europe* (1911) ; *The Age of Grey and Peel* (ed. G. M. Trevelyan, 1929).

FIGGIS, JOHN NEVILLE [1866–1919], historian and divine.

For life and works see *Dictionary National Biography, Supplement, 1912–21*. Some of his best writing is in *The Divine Right of Kings* (1896) ; *From Gerson to Grotius* (1907) ; "Political Thought in the Sixteenth Century" (in *Cambridge Modern History*, Vol. III., chap. 22. (1907)) ; *Churches in the Modern State* (1913) ; *The Political Aspects of St. Augustine's De Civitate Dei* (1921).

FIRTH, SIR CHARLES HARDING [1857–1936], Regius Professor of Modern History in the University of Oxford.

For an estimate of his work see E. S. de Beer, "Sir Charles Firth, 1857–1936" (in *History*, N.S. XXI. (June 1936), pp. 1–13). A list of his publications is in C. H. FIRTH, *A Bibliography of the Writings of Sir Charles Firth* (1928). Of his books the most important are *Oliver Cromwell and the Rule of the Puritans in England* (1900) ; *Cromwell's Army* (1902) ; *The Last Years of the Protectorate, 1656–58* (1909) ; *The House of Lords during the Civil War* (1910) ; *A Plea for the*

Historical Teaching of History (1904). See also " The Undeserved Neglect of Earlier English Historians by their Successors" (in *Bulletin of the Institute of Historical Research*, V. 65–69 (1923), and *Essays Historical and Literary* (1938).

FISHER, HERBERT ALBERT LAURENS, Warden of New College, Oxford.

Historical works include *The Mediæval Empire* (1898) ; *Studies in Napoleonic Statesmanship* (1903) ; *The Political History of England, 1485–1547* (1906) ; *The Republican Tradition in Europe* (1911) ; *Napoleon* (1912) ; *Studies in History and Politics* (1920) ; *Whig Historians* (1928) ; *A History of Europe* (1935).

FORTESCUE, SIR JOHN [1859–1933].

His main work is *The History of the British Army*, 13 vols. (1899–1930), but he published many volumes of essays including *Historical and Military Essays* (1928), *The Writing of History* (1926), and *British Statesmen of the Great War, 1793–1814* (1921).

GOOCH, GEORGE PEABODY.

Of great importance as an introduction to modern historiography is his *History and Historians in the Nineteenth Century* (1913). Other works include *English Democratic Ideas in the Seventeenth Century* (1898, new ed. 1927) ; *A History of Modern Europe, 1878–1919* (1923) ; *Studies in Modern History* (1931).

GUEDALLA, PHILIP.

The Second Empire (1922, revised ed. 1932) ; *Palmerston* (1926) ; *Collected Essays* (1927) ; *The Missing Muse and Other Essays* (1929).

HAVERFIELD, FRANCIS JOHN [1860–1919], Camden Professor of Ancient History in the University of Oxford.

For an appreciation see G. Macdonald, *Francis Haverfield* (1921), and G. Macdonald's memoir in the revised edition of Haverfield, *Roman Occupation of Britain* (1924). Other works include " Roman Britain " (in *Cambridge Mediæval History*, Vol. I., chap. 13.) ; *The Romanization of Roman Britain* (1906, new ed. 1923) ; *The Study of Ancient History in Oxford* (1912).

BIBLIOGRAPHY

HODGKIN, THOMAS [1831–1913], banker and historian.

For life see *Dictionary National Biography, Supplement*, II., and L. Creighton, *Life and Letters of Thomas Hodgkin* (1917). Works include *Italy and Her Invaders*, 8 vols. (1880–99) ; *The Dynasty of Theodosius* (1889) ; *Theodoric the Goth* (1891) ; *Charles the Great* (1897) ; *History of England from the Earliest Times to the Norman Conquest* (1906).

KINGSFORD, CHARLES LETHBRIDGE [1862–1926].

For an account of his work see E. Jeffries Davis, " The Work of C. L. Kingsford " (in *London Topographical Record*, Vol. XIV. (1928), pp. 58–80, with a bibliography of his work relating to London history, and A. G. Little, *Charles Kingsford* (1927). His more general historical writings include *Henry V.* (1901) ; *English Historical Literature in the Fifteenth Century* (1913) ; *Prejudice and Promise in Fifteenth Century England* (1925) ; " The Kingdom of Jerusalem, 1099–1291 " (in *Cambridge Mediæval History*, Vol. V., chap. 8.).

MAITLAND, FREDERICK WILLIAM [1850–1906], Downing Professor of the Laws of England in the University of Cambridge.

For life see A. L. Smith, *Frederick William Maitland* (1908) ; H. A. L. Fisher, *F. W. Maitland* (1910) ; and *Dictionary National Biography, Supplement 1901–11.* The best known of his historical writings : *The History of English Law Before the Time of Edward I.* (1895) ; *Domesday Book and Beyond* (1897) ; *Township and Borough* (1898) ; *Roman Canon Law in the Church of England* (1898) ; *Political Theories of the Middle Ages* (1900) ; *Life and Letters of Leslie Stephen* (1906) ; " The Elizabethan Settlement " (in *Cambridge Modern History*, Vol. II., chap. 16). For a selection of his essays see *The Collected Papers of Frederick William Maitland* (ed. H. A. L. Fisher, 3 vols., 1911) and *Selected Essays* (ed. P. H. Winfield, G. Lapsley, and H. D. Hazeltine, 1936).

POLLARD, ALBERT FREDERICK, sometime Professor of History in the University of London ; Hon. Director of the Institute of Historical Research, University of London.

Works include *England under Protector Somerset* (1900) ; *Henry VIII.* (1902, 1905) ; *Thomas Cranmer* (1904) ; *Factors in Modern History* (1907) ; *The Political History of England, 1547-1603* (1910) ; *History of England* (1912) ; *The Evolution of Parliament* (1920) ; *Wolsey* (1929). Among numerous essays is one of special interest to students of modern historical method— " An Essay in Historical Method : The Barbellion Diaries " (in *History*, N.S. VI. (April 1921), pp. 23-31, and *ibid.* (Oct. 1921), pp. 183-194).

POWELL, FREDERICK YORK [1850-1904], Regius Professor of Modern History in the University of Oxford.

For life and works consult the memoir (with collection of essays) by Oliver Elton, *Frederick York Powell*, 2 vols. (1906).

POWER, EILEEN, Professor of Economic History in the University of London.

For works see *The Paycockes of Coggeshill* (1920) ; *Mediæval English Nunneries* (1922) ; *Mediæval People* (1924) ; *The Goodman of Paris* (translated with an introduction, (1928) ; " Peasant Life and Rural Conditions (*c.* 1100 to *c.* 1500) " (in *Cambridge Mediæval History*, Vol. VII., chap. 24).

POWICKE, FREDERICK MAURICE, Regius Professor of Modern History in the University of Oxford.

His writings include the following : *The Loss of Normandy* (1913) ; *Ailred of Rievaulx* (1922) ; *Stephen Langton* (1928) ; *Historical Study in Oxford* (1929) ; " England : Richard I. and John," " The Reigns of Philip Augustus and Louis VIII. of France " (in *Cambridge Mediæval History*, VI., c. 7 and 9) ; *Mediæval England* (1931) ; *The Christian Life in the Middle Ages and Other Essays* (1935).

RALEIGH, SIR WALTER [1861-1922], Professor of English Literature in the University of Oxford.

For life and works see Gwen Violet, *Sir Walter Alexander Raleigh* (1923) and *The Letters of Sir Walter Raleigh* (ed. Lady Raleigh, 1926 ; 1928). Works include *The English Voyages of the Sixteenth Century* (1910) ; *The*

War in the Air, Vol. I. (1922), the official history of the Royal Air Force.

STENTON, FRANK MERRY, Professor of Modern History in the University of Reading.

Besides his work for the Place Name Society and other technical works, his writings include *William the Conqueror and the Rule of the Normans* (1890) ; *The Danes in England* (1928) ; *The First Century of English Feudalism* (1932).

TAWNEY, RICHARD HENRY, Professor of Economic History in the University of London.

Historical writing includes *The Agrarian Problem in the Sixteenth Century* (1912) ; *The Acquisitive Society* (1921) ; *A Discourse upon Usury by Thomas Wilson* (1925) ; *Studies in Economic History* (see below, under George Unwin) ; *Religion and the Rise of Capitalism* (1926).

TEMPERLEY, HAROLD WILLIAM VAZELLE, Professor of History in the University of Cambridge.

Works include a *History of Serbia* (1917) ; *History of the Peace Conference of Paris*, 6 vols (1920–24) ; *Life of Canning* (1905) ; *The Victorian Age in Politics, War, and Diplomacy* (1928) ; *Selected Essays of J. B. Bury* (with an introduction, 1930) ; *Research and Modern History* (1930) ; *Foreign Historical Novels* (1929).

THOMPSON, ALEXANDER HAMILTON, Professor of Mediæval History in the University of Leeds.

Works include *Historical Growth of the English Parish Church* (1911) ; *Military Architecture in England in the Middle Ages* (1912) ; *English Monasteries* (1913) ; *The Cathedral Churches of England* (1925).

TOUT, THOMAS FREDERICK [1855–1929], Professor of History in the University of Manchester.

For life and estimates of his work see F. M. Powicke's memoir in *The Collected Papers of Thomas Frederick Tout* and A. G. Little (in *History*, Vol. XIV., January 1930, pp. 313–24). Bibliography in *Collected Papers*, Vol. I., p. 207 (and see note, p. 22). Books include *Edward I.* (1893) ; *The Empire and Papacy* (1898) ; *The Political History of England, 1216–1377* (1905) ;

The Place of the Reign of Edward II. in English History (1914) ; *Chapters in the Administrative History of Mediæval England,* 6 vols. (1920–35).

TOYNBEE, ARNOLD J., Director of Studies in the Royal Institute of International Affairs and Research Professor of International History in the University of London.

His main historical work consists of *The Place of Mediæval and Modern Greece in History* (1919) ; *The Western Question in Greece and Turkey* (1922) ; *The World After the Peace Conference* (1925) ; *Survey of International Politics, 1920–23* (1925), and continuations ; *A Study of History* (first three volumes, 1934).

TREVELYAN, GEORGE MACAULAY, Regius Professor of Modern History in the University of Cambridge.

Works include *England in the Age of Wycliffe* (1899) ; *England Under the Stuarts* (1904) ; *Garibaldi's Defence of the Roman Republic* (1907) ; *Garibaldi and the Thousand* (1909) ; *Garibaldi and the Making of Italy* (1916); *Clio: a Muse, and Other Essays* (1913)—reprinted with additions as *The Recreations of an Historian* (1919) ; *History of England* (1926) ; *British History in the Nineteenth Century* (1922) ; *England Under Queen Anne,* 3 vols. (1930–34) ; *The Present Position of History* (1927).

UNWIN, GEORGE [1870–1925], Professor of Economic History in the University of Manchester.

For life, critical estimate, and bibliography consult *Studies in Economic History : The Collected Papers of George Unwin* (ed. R. H. Tawney (1927). Of Unwin's books the outstanding ones are *Industrial Organization in the Sixteenth and Seventeenth Centuries* (1904) ; *The Gilds and Companies of London* (1908) ; *Samuel Oldknow and the Arkwrights* ; but much of his best work is in the form of essays and reviews, for which see the *Collected Papers.*

VINOGRADOFF, SIR PAUL [1854–1925], Corpus Professor of Jurisprudence in the University of Oxford.

For life and bibliography see H. A. L. Fisher, *Collected Papers of Sir Paul Vinogradov,* 2 vols. (1928), and

BIBLIOGRAPHY

Holdsworth, W. S., *Professor Paul Vinogradoff* (1926). Of his works the best known are *Villeinage in England* (1892) ; *English Society in the Eleventh Century* (1908) ; *Growth of the Manor* (1905) ; *Outlines of Historical Jurisprudence* (1926) ; *Roman Law in Mediæval Europe* (1909 ; second edition edited by F. de Zulveta, 1929).

PRINTED IN GREAT BRITAIN AT
THE PRESS OF THE PUBLISHERS